INVESTING
DECIPHERED

Basics to Brilliance

Harshal Patil

ISBN - Paperback : 9-798-3942-5219-8

First Edition : May 2023

LIMITS AND LIABILITY

This book, crafted with diligence and care, aims to provide valuable information on the subject matter covered. It is, however, essential to clarify that neither the author nor the publisher are offering legal, financial, or other professional services. Should you require expert assistance, the services of a competent professional should be sought. While every effort has been made to ensure the accuracy of the information contained herein, neither the author nor the publisher can be held responsible for any errors or omissions. The content is presented 'as is', with the reader bearing the responsibility for its use.

Investing inherently involves risks, including potential financial loss. The strategies discussed in this book do not guarantee success, and the author cannot be held accountable for any financial losses or damages incurred from the use of this information. The book is not a substitute for professional advice. It is incumbent upon investors to conduct their own research and consult a qualified financial advisor before making financial decisions. This book does not offer personalized financial or investment advice or solicit any securities or financial instruments.

By engaging with this book, you acknowledge and accept these terms and conditions, agreeing to hold the author and publisher harmless from any claims or liabilities that may arise from your use of the information herein. The author reserves the right to update the book's content at any time, with changes incorporated in new editions of the publication.

Use this information responsibly and wisely.

About the author

Harshal has a wealth of experience spanning over 15 years of actively and successfully trading and investing in various investment vehicles; such as stocks, mutual funds, ETFs, and derivatives like options. In addition, he has gained valuable exposure to the private equity sector, engaging with a diverse array of companies across venture capital, buyout funds, and fund-of-funds spaces. These experiences have equipped the author with invaluable insights into the realm of investing, which are now being shared through this book.

Throughout this extensive tenure in the financial industry, the author has come to appreciate the significance of meticulous research, risk management, and diversification in the investment process. Personally, witnessing the potential rewards of informed and strategic investment choices has emphasized the indispensability of continuous learning in the ever-changing landscape of investing.

Driven by a passion for inspiring others in making astute and well-informed investment decisions, the author believes that financial literacy is an essential skill for anyone seeking to safeguard their financial future. With the intention of introducing investments to novices and enhancing the knowledge of those already familiar with the domain, this book has been crafted to serve both audiences in a concise and informative manner. Through the insights and guidance provided, the author aims to help individuals navigate the intricacies of investing and attain their financial objectives.

Table of Contents

PART III: INVESTING IN SPECIFIC ASSET CLASSES

PART IV: ADVANCED INVESTMENT STRATEGIES

PART V: INVESTMENT TOOLS AND TECHNIQUES

PART VI: GETTING STARTED

Part I

Introduction to Investments

Chapter 1

What is Investing?

An Art, Science and a Crucial Part of Human Civilization

Investing is a timeless craft that has been intricately woven into the tapestry of human history, from the early days of bartering to the complex financial instruments of today's markets. Often viewed as both an art and a science, investing requires a blend of analytical rigor and imaginative finesse to navigate the ever-evolving landscape of opportunities. While the science of investing involves analyzing financial data, identifying trends, and making predictions based on past performance, the art of investing involves creativity, intuition, and an ability to perceive what lies beyond the numbers. Through the centuries, investing has played a vital role in driving economic growth and creating wealth for individuals and societies alike.

At its core, investing is about making decisions based on imperfect information, balancing risk and reward, and adapting to changing market conditions. These are not easy tasks, and successful investors must possess a combination of technical skills and emotional intelligence to navigate the ups and downs of the market.

The art of investing involves the ability to see opportunities where others do not, to identify undervalued assets, and to have the courage to make bold moves when necessary. It also requires an understanding of human psychology and the ability to control one's own emotions in the face of market volatility.

Besides, investing is not just about making money. It is also about creating a portfolio that aligns with an investor's values and goals. This may involve investing in companies that are making a positive impact on society or circumventing investments in industries that go against an investor's values.

In retrospect, investing is an enduring art, crafted over time, refined and redefined with each passing age. In today's dynamic world, replete with new technologies and opportunities, investors are presented with a wealth of options, spanning from the traditional to the avant-garde. The secret to triumph in this world of investments lies in comprehending the varied types of investments and the approaches that thriving investors use to reap long-term gains. As we embark on this chapter, let us immerse ourselves in the history of investing, explore the bedrock principles that prop up flourishing investments, and uncover the vast and varied investment options available to present-day investors.

Origins and History of Investing

The history of investing is a story that spans centuries, dating back to the earliest forms of trade and commerce in various civilizations. The Mauryan Empire in ancient India traded goods and services, which evolved into the use of punch-marked coins as a medium of exchange, facilitating organized trade and the emergence of marketplaces. Similarly, ancient Egypt saw trade in goods like wheat, barley, and papyrus lead to the development of marketplaces.

Fast forward to the 1600s, the Dutch East India Company was one of the most successful trading companies in the world, and it wanted to raise capital for its business ventures. To do so, it began issuing shares of stock, allowing investors to buy a stake in the company and participate in its profits. The company even paid out dividends, which were a portion of its profits that it distributed to its shareholders. This system was so successful that it gave birth to the world's first stock exchange, the Amsterdam Stock Exchange.

As the popularity of stocks grew, other countries began to establish their own stock exchanges, such as the London Stock Exchange in 1801 and the New York Stock Exchange in 1817. Stock exchanges provided investors with a centralized marketplace to buy and sell stocks, providing liquidity and increasing market efficiency.

As trade became more systematized, early investors began to finance explorations and expeditions in exchange for a share of the profits. These early investors took on a considerable amount of risk, but the potential rewards were enormous. They were the pioneers of modern-day investing, and they set the foundation for the financial markets we know today.

In the 20th century, the financial markets continued to evolve, with the introduction of new financial instruments and trading technologies. The development of mutual funds in the 1920s allowed smaller investors to pool their resources and access a diverse range of investments. The introduction of computerized trading systems in the 1970s and 1980s led to increased speed and efficiency in trading, paving the way for the electronic trading platforms that dominate the markets today.

In recent years, the rise of technology has disrupted traditional investment models, giving birth to new asset classes such as cryptocurrencies and alternative investments. The use of artificial intelligence and machine learning has also revolutionized investment analysis and decision-making.

To synthesize, investing has played a crucial role in human civilization for centuries, progressing from rudimentary bartering and trading to an intricate network of financial markets and investment instruments. Despite numerous transformations, the core principles of investing persist; generating returns by allocating resources to diverse assets and asset classes, while striking a balance between risk and reward. Comprehending the history of investing can yield invaluable insights into the underpinnings of investing and the strategies that have culminated in long-term success.

Fundamental Concepts of Investing

Investing is an intricate dominion that demands a profound comprehension of its fundamental concepts to thrive. At its essence, investing involves entrusting capital into an enterprise or asset with the anticipation of reaping a return on the investment. Yet, the art of investing encompasses much more than a simple transaction, and prosperous investors must possess an array of skills and knowledge. From market analysis to risk management, the world of investing requires astute attention to detail and a well-rounded understanding of economic trends and financial principles.

Risk-return trade-off: In general, the higher the risk of an investment, the greater the potential return, and the lower the risk, the lower the potential return. The risk-return trade-off is a fundamental concept that drives investment decisions and is the primary factor in determining an investor's overall portfolio strategy.

Risk management: Risk management is a crucial aspect of investing, and understanding how to manage risk is essential for long-term success. A key principle of risk management is diversification, which involves spreading investments across a range of assets and asset classes. By diversifying your portfolio, you can minimize the impact of any one investment's poor performance on your overall returns.

Asset allocation: Asset allocation refers to the process of dividing investments among various asset classes, such as stocks, bonds, and real estate, based on an investor's risk tolerance, investment goals, and time horizon. Asset allocation is a key factor in achieving a balanced portfolio that generates consistent returns while minimizing risk.

Liquidity: Liquidity refers to the ease with which an asset can be bought or sold without significantly affecting its price. More liquid assets, such as stocks and bonds, can be bought and sold easily, while less liquid assets, such as real estate or private equity, can be more challenging to sell quickly.

Taxes and inflation: Investors should be aware of the impact of taxes and inflation on their investments. Taxes can eat into returns, so it's important to consider the tax implications of any investment decisions. Similarly, inflation can erode the purchasing power of returns over time, so investors need to consider the rate of inflation when evaluating their investment returns.

Market efficiency: Market efficiency is the degree to which prices of securities reflect all available information. In other words, if the market is efficient, it is difficult to find undervalued or overvalued securities, and it's challenging to consistently outperform the market. Understanding market efficiency is critical to the success of active investment strategies, such as stock picking and market timing.

Compounding: Compounding is essential for long-term investors. Compounding refers to the process of reinvesting investment returns to generate more significant returns over time. By reinvesting returns, investors can take advantage of the power of compounding, which can significantly increase their wealth over the long term.

Ultimately, surmounting these foundational principles is essential for investors aiming to achieve enduring success. Armed with an in-depth understanding of these notions, individuals can make discerning investment choices that align with their financial goals and risk tolerance. As the investment landscape perpetually transforms, maintaining up-to-date knowledge and education on core concepts is vital for thriving in this enthralling arena.

Types of Investments

The universe of investments is a vast and dynamic landscape that beckons to investors seeking to build their wealth. From traditional investments like stocks and bonds to newer, more innovative options like cryptocurrencies and alternative assets, the types of investments available to investors are as varied as they are complex. In this section, we will delve into the world of investments and provide a brief overview of some of the most common types of investments.

In Part III and IV, we shall delve into the intricacies of each investment type, except for alternative assets like private equity, as they are beyond the scope of this book.

Stocks: Stocks represent ownership in a company and are one of the most common types of investments. When you buy a stock, you become a shareholder in the company, and you are entitled to a portion of the company's profits. Several established companies typically distribute profits to shareholders in the form of dividends, which are paid out regularly. Alternatively, investors can realize a return on their investment through capital gains, which occur when the stock price rises above the purchase price.

Investors can purchase stocks through stock exchanges or through online brokerage platforms. The value of stocks can fluctuate based on a wide range of factors, including but not limited to market trends, industry performance, and company-specific news.

Bonds: Bonds are debt securities issued by companies and governments to raise capital. When you buy a bond, you are effectively lending money to the issuer, and in return, the issuer promises to pay you a fixed interest rate for the life of the bond. Bonds can be a relatively low-risk investment, as they provide a predictable income stream and are typically less volatile than stocks. However, the potential returns on bonds are generally lower than those of stocks.

There are many different types of bonds available, including government bonds, corporate bonds, and municipal bonds. Investors can purchase bonds through brokerage firms or online trading platforms.

Mutual Funds: Mutual funds are investment vehicles that pool money from multiple investors to purchase a diversified portfolio of assets, such as stocks, bonds, and other securities. By investing in a mutual fund, investors gain exposure to a variety of different asset classes.

Mutual funds are typically managed by professional fund managers who make investment decisions on behalf of the fund's investors. Investors can buy and sell mutual fund shares like stocks, and the value of the mutual fund is determined by the performance of the underlying assets.

Exchange-Traded Funds (ETFs): ETFs are similar to mutual funds in that they offer investors exposure to a diversified portfolio of assets. However, ETFs are traded on stock exchanges like stocks, which makes them more flexible and easier to trade than mutual funds. ETFs also tend to have lower fees than mutual funds, making them an attractive option for cost-conscious investors.

Like mutual funds, ETFs invest in a variety of different asset classes, including stocks, bonds, and commodities. The value of an ETF is determined by the performance of the underlying assets.

Commodities: Commodities are raw materials or primary agricultural products that are traded in bulk, such as oil, gold, or wheat. Investing in commodities can be a way to diversify a portfolio and potentially hedge against inflation, as commodity prices tend to rise during times of inflation. However, investing in commodities can be risky and volatile, as prices are influenced by a variety of factors such as global supply and demand, weather conditions, and geopolitical events.

Derivatives: Derivatives are financial instruments that derive their value from an underlying asset or security, such as a stock, bond, or commodity. Examples of derivatives include futures, options, and swaps. Derivatives can be used by investors to speculate on the future price of an asset or to hedge against potential losses. However, derivatives can be complex and carry a high level of risk, and should only be traded by experienced investors.

Cryptocurrencies: Cryptocurrencies are digital or virtual tokens that use cryptography to secure and verify transactions and to control the creation of new units. Bitcoin, Ethereum, and other cryptocurrencies have gained significant attention in recent years due to their potential as a decentralized and anonymous form of currency. Investing in cryptocurrencies can be highly speculative and volatile, as the value of these digital assets is influenced by a variety of factors such as market sentiment, regulatory developments, and technological advancements.

Alternative Assets: Alternative assets are an asset class that fall outside of traditional asset classes such as stocks, bonds, and real estate. Examples of alternative assets include private equity, venture capital, hedge funds, and art or collectibles. Alternative assets can be attractive to investors seeking higher returns or diversification, but they can also be illiquid, complex, and require significant due diligence and expertise. These types of investments can be high-risk and often require significant capital investments.

In essence, the contemporary investor has access to a vast array of investment opportunities, each presenting its distinct advantages and risks. By comprehending the diverse types of investments and the strategies employed by proficient investors, individuals can make judicious decisions that resonate with their financial objectives and risk appetite.

Summary

Tracing back to ancient times, the history of investing began with simple exchanges of goods and services, eventually sprouting into a refined practice necessitating knowledge and skill. The inception of the Amsterdam stock exchange in the 1600s heralded a crucial shift, laying the foundation for contemporary financial markets.

Investing entails managing risk and pursuing returns on investment. Prosperous investors hold a profound grasp of essential concepts such as risk-return trade-off, diversification, and asset allocation. A myriad of investment options allows investors to construct diversified portfolios that resonate with their financial objectives and risk appetite.

Investing is not a shortcut to wealth; it demands discipline, patience, and a long-term outlook. While the assortment of investment types and strategies for success can appear daunting, the right knowledge and guidance enable investors to make well-informed decisions, fostering financial stability and wealth generation.

In the subsequent chapters, we will delve into every investment option in-depth, presenting a comprehensive overview of the strategies employed by successful investors.

Chapter 2

Key Theories and Models in Finance

The world of finance is dynamic, continuously in motion, and always seeking to uncover new insights to guide investors through the uncertainties of the market. As a result, several schools of thought have emerged, each playing a vital role in the financial universe. This chapter is dedicated to the exploration of the four main theories and models that have shaped modern finance: Behavioral Finance, Modern Portfolio Theory, the Efficient Market Hypothesis, and the Capital Asset Pricing Model.

Behavioral Finance

Behavioral Finance is a relatively new area of finance that seeks to understand how human psychology and emotions impact financial decision-making behavior. Traditional finance models often assume that investors behave rationally, but Behavioral Finance acknowledges that emotions and biases can lead to irrational decision-making. This theory draws on insights not only from psychology but also sociology, and other social sciences to help explain why investors sometimes make suboptimal decisions.

Some key insights from Behavioral Finance include the recognition of cognitive biases such as loss aversion, overconfidence, and herd behavior, which can lead to poor investment decisions. In addition, the field has identified several common heuristics or shortcuts that people use to make decisions, which can lead to poor judgment in certain circumstances. Perhaps, by understanding these psychological biases, investors can better assess the risks and potential rewards of different investment options.

Example: Loss aversion is an investor cognitive bias where they are more sensitive to the pain of loss than to the prospect or joy of gain. This can cause investors to hold onto losing investments for too long, in the hope that they will eventually recover, instead of selling them and moving on to other opportunities.

Modern Portfolio Theory

Modern Portfolio Theory (MPT) is a foundational theory in finance that has been used for decades to help investors optimize their portfolios. Developed by economist Harry Markowitz, MPT proposes that investors can maximize returns while minimizing risk by investing in a diverse portfolio of assets. The theory assumes that investors are rational, risk-averse, and looking to maximize their returns, given a certain level of risk.

MPT proposes that investors should diversify their investments across multiple asset classes, such as stocks, bonds, and real estate, in order to reduce their exposure to risk. By investing in a diversified portfolio, investors can potentially earn higher returns with lower risk, rather than by investing in any single asset class.

Example: Investing in a single stock is like putting all your eggs in one basket. If that stock performs poorly, your entire portfolio is at risk. Diversifying your portfolio by investing in multiple stocks across different industries can reduce your risk and potentially improve your returns. Just like a farmer planting a variety of crops to ensure a good harvest, a diversified portfolio can help ensure a healthy investment portfolio.

Efficient Market Hypothesis

Efficient Market Hypothesis (EMH) is a theory that suggests that financial markets are highly efficient and that stock prices always reflect all available information. The theory assumes that investors are rational and that the market is highly competitive, meaning that it is difficult to consistently outperform the market. The EMH also suggests that stock prices follow a random walk pattern, making it impossible to predict future stock prices based on past performance.

The EMH has significant implications for investors, as it suggests that attempting to beat the market through stock picking or market timing is unlikely to be successful. Instead, investors who believe in the EMH typically opt for passive investment strategies such as index funds, which track the performance of an entire market rather than attempting to beat it.

Example: The stock market is like a giant auction house where buyers and sellers come together to exchange shares of companies. In an efficient market, all buyers and sellers have access to the same information about the companies being traded, and the market quickly incorporates that information into the price of the stock. Trying to outsmart the market by picking individual stocks or timing the market is like trying to win an auction against thousands of other bidders - it's ambiguous. Instead, investors can focus on building a diversified portfolio of low-cost index funds that track the market.

Capital Asset Pricing Model

Capital Asset Pricing Model (CAPM) is a model used to calculate the expected return on an investment based on the asset's risk level. The model assumes that there is a risk-free rate of return, and that investors demand a higher return for taking on additional risk. CAPM uses this information to calculate the expected return on an investment based on its level of risk.

The CAPM has important practical implications for investors, as it suggests that higher-risk investments should offer higher returns than lower-risk investments. By assessing the risk and expected return of different investment options, investors can use the CAPM to make informed investment decisions.

Example: Investing in a high-growth, high-risk technology stock is like riding a roller coaster - it can be exhilarating, but also nerve-wracking. The CAPM helps investors understand the risk and potential reward of each stock in their portfolio. Just like a roller coaster, a high-risk stock should offer a higher expected return than a low-risk stock. By understanding the risk and reward of each stock in their portfolio, investors can make informed decisions about how much risk they're willing to take on in pursuit of higher returns.

Summary

The sphere of finance is vast and ever-shifting, and the theories we've explored here are merely a glimpse of its complexity. Yet, by delving into these core concepts, investors can gain a sturdy foundation for wise investment choices. Behavioral Finance illuminates the vital role of human behavior and biases in financial decision-making, while Modern Portfolio Theory emphasizes the power of diversification in reducing risk. Efficient Market Hypothesis posits that all available information is reflected in the market's current price, making it challenging to consistently outperform the market, and the Capital Asset Pricing Model provides a framework for understanding the interplay between risk and reward.

These theories and models empower investors to design effective investment strategies and make sound investment decisions. But they are not infallible, and investors should exercise caution and perform their own research and analysis before investing.

As finance continues to evolve, new theories and models will emerge, and investors must stay abreast of the latest developments to stay ahead of the game.

Chapter 3

Investment Strategies

Investment, the artful and scientific pursuit, seeks to build wealth by shrewdly allocating resources. Amidst a multitude of investment options, the task of discerning the most fruitful strategies can prove challenging. Two widely embraced approaches are growth and value investing. In this chapter, we shall delve into the depths of these and additional investment principles, exploring their nuances, benefits, and potential pitfalls.

Growth Investing

Growth investing, a strategy beloved by those with a penchant for forward-thinking, involves identifying and investing in companies expected to experience rapid growth in the future.

Key points to understand about growth investing:

- Growth investors prioritize companies with the potential for outpacing market growth. These companies may belong to sectors experiencing rapid growth, such as technology or healthcare. Alternatively, they may be enterprises exhibiting strong growth propelled by new products or services.

- Growth investors understand the higher levels of risk associated with this strategy, but are willing to assume them in the hope of higher returns. Growth companies, being less established, are often more volatile and lack a track record of stability.

- Employing a variety of strategies, growth investors analyze individual companies and industries, scrutinize financial statements and market trends, and seek counsel from financial professionals to identify potential investment opportunities.

- This approach is best suited to investors with a long-term time horizon and a higher tolerance for risk in exchange for the potential for higher returns.

Examples of companies that may be considered growth investments:

Technology companies: Companies in the technology sector, such as software and hardware developers, may be considered growth investments due to the rapid pace of innovation in the industry. For example, Apple Inc. is a technology company that has consistently experienced strong growth due to the success of its products, such as the iPhone and iPad.

Healthcare companies: Companies in the healthcare sector, such as pharmaceutical and biotech firms, may be considered growth investments due to the increasing demand for healthcare services and innovative treatments. For example, Moderna Inc. is a biotech company that has experienced strong growth due to its innovative work in developing vaccines and other therapies.

Consumer goods companies: Companies that produce consumer goods, such as clothing and consumer electronics, may be considered growth investments if they are able to consistently introduce new and popular products. For example, Nike Inc. is a consumer goods company that has experienced strong growth due to its innovative products and strong brand recognition.

Service companies: Service companies, such as consulting and professional services firms, may be considered growth investments if they are able to consistently increase their client base and revenue. For example, Deloitte is a professional services firm that has experienced strong growth due to its expertise in a variety of industries and its ability to attract and retain clients.

Value Investing

Value investing, a style of investing that seeks to identify undervalued companies, offers investors the potential to realize a profit when the market eventually recognizes a company's true value.

Key points to understand about value investing:

- This investment strategy involves focusing on fundamental analysis, including a company's financial statements, management team, and competitive landscape, to determine its intrinsic value. Additionally, macroeconomic and industry trends, as well as a company's growth potential and future prospects, may also be considered when evaluating potential investment opportunities.

- Value investors typically have a long-term time horizon and are willing to hold onto their investments for extended periods of time, with the belief that the market will eventually recognize the true value of the company and the price will increase.

Examples of companies that may be considered value investments:

Companies in industries that are out of favor: Companies in industries that are experiencing difficult times or are out of favor with investors may be considered value investments if they are able to weather the storm and have a strong fundamental value. For example, General Motors is a company that was considered a value investment after it emerged from bankruptcy in 2009 and began restructuring its operations.

Companies with strong financials: Companies that have strong financials, such as a low price-to-earnings ratio or a strong balance sheet, may be considered value investments if they are trading at a discount to their intrinsic value. For example, Goldman Sachs is a financial services company that has a strong balance sheet.

Companies with a strong brand or competitive advantage: Companies that have a strong brand or a competitive advantage in their industry may be considered value investments if they are trading at a discount to their intrinsic value. For example, Coca-Cola is a consumer goods company with a strong brand and a competitive advantage due to its distribution network and wide range of products.

Companies with a solid track record: Companies with a solid track record of financial performance may be considered value investments if they are trading at a discount to their intrinsic value. For example, Johnson & Johnson is a healthcare company with a long history of strong financial performance.

Income Investing

Income investing is a prudent investment approach that prioritizes investments that offer a regular income stream. This can be achieved through dividends, interest payments, or other similar avenues.

Key points to understand about income investing:

- Investors seeking to adopt this approach prioritize investments that offer a high yield, or a high rate of return relative to the investment's price. This could mean investing in dividend-paying stocks, bond funds, or real estate investment trusts (REITs).

- Income investors may be seeking a reliable source of income to supplement their retirement savings or to meet their current financial needs. Thus, this investment approach can be particularly attractive to investors who are risk-averse.

- Income investing is a strategy that can be suitable for investors who prioritize a predictable and consistent stream of income over the potential for capital appreciation.

- It is crucial to note that income investing comes with its own set of risks, such as the risk of default on bonds or a decline in the value of the stock. Thus, investors must carefully evaluate their financial goals, risk tolerance, and time horizon before adopting this strategy.

Examples of investments that may be considered income investments:

Dividend-paying stocks: Companies that consistently pay dividends to their shareholders may be considered income investments. For example, utilities companies, such as Duke Energy, are often considered income investments due to their consistent dividend payments.

Bond funds: Bond funds are investments that pool together the assets of multiple bonds and offer investors the opportunity to earn income through interest payments. For example, the Vanguard Total Bond Market ETF is a bond fund that offers a diversified portfolio of bonds and a relatively high yield.

REITs: REITs are investment trusts that own and operate real estate properties and offer investors the opportunity to earn income through dividends and capital appreciation. For example, the Vanguard Real Estate ETF is a REIT that offers a diversified portfolio of real estate properties and a relatively high yield.

Savings accounts: Savings accounts are a low-risk investment option that offer a predictable source of income through interest payments. For example, a high-yield savings account at an online bank may offer a relatively high yield compared to a traditional brick-and-mortar bank.

Day Trading

Day trading is a fast-paced and high-risk style of investing that involves buying and selling securities within a single trading day, with the aim of making a profit from short-term price movements.

Key points to understand about day trading:

- To be a successful day trader, one must have a deep understanding of the markets and the ability to quickly analyze and act on market trends, technical analysis tools, and news events.

- Day traders often use leverage to increase potential profits, but this also amplifies the risks associated with their trades.

- It is crucial to note that day trading requires a significant level of skill, expertise, and discipline. Day traders must be able to make swift and cognisant decisions, and continuously monitor the markets for opportunities. Additionally, day trading can be a time-consuming and stressful activity that requires a high level of liquidity, which may not be suitable for all investors.

- Before engaging in day trading, investors should carefully consider their financial goals, risk tolerance, and time horizon. They should also have a well-thought-out trading plan that takes into account the risks and potential returns associated with their trades. Only those who are willing to accept the high level of risk and devote the necessary time and resources to it should consider day trading as a strategy.

Examples of securities that day traders may focus on:

Stocks: Day traders may focus on stocks, particularly those that are highly liquid and have a high degree of price volatility. For example, a day trader may focus on stocks in the technology sector, such as Apple Inc. or Amazon.com, as these companies tend to be highly liquid and may experience significant price movements due to market trends or news events.

Options: Options are financial instruments that give the holder the right, but not the obligation, to buy or sell a security at a predetermined price. Day traders may focus on options, as they offer the potential for significant profits in a short period of time. For example, a day trader may focus on options on stocks in the technology sector, such as Nvidia.

Foreign exchange (forex): The forex market involves the buying and selling of currencies. It is highly liquid and open 24 hours a day, making it a popular choice for day traders. For example, a day trader may focus on currency pairs such as the U.S. dollar versus the euro or the U.S. dollar versus the Japanese yen.

Commodities: Commodities, such as gold or oil, may also be of interest to day traders due to their high liquidity and potential for price movements due to market trends or geopolitical events.

Swing Trading

Swing trading is a sophisticated investment approach that aims to capitalize on short-term price movements in securities. Unlike day trading, which involves buying and selling securities within a single trading day, swing traders hold onto their positions for several days to a few weeks. The goal is to capture significant price movements during this period, which can be achieved by carefully selecting securities that are likely to experience such fluctuations.

Key points to understand about swing trading:

- To identify potential trades, swing traders use a variety of strategies, including analyzing market trends, technical analysis tools, and news events. However, this requires a high level of skill and expertise, as well as the ability to make quick and informed decisions. As such, swing trading is not suitable for all investors and carries a high level of risk.

- In terms of liquidity, swing traders require a moderate level to enter and exit trades quickly, but not to the same extent as day traders. Nevertheless, swing trading can also be a time-consuming and stressful activity, as it involves continuously monitoring the markets and making rapid-fire decisions. Therefore, it should only be undertaken by those who are willing to accept the risks and can devote the necessary time and resources to it.

- To be successful in swing trading, it is crucial to have a well-thought-out trading plan and to carefully consider the risks and potential rewards of each trade. This requires discipline and patience, as well as the ability to adapt to changing market conditions. Overall, swing trading can be a highly rewarding investment approach for those who are willing to put in the necessary effort and have the right skills and expertise.

Examples of a day and swing trading process:

Identifying a trend: The first step in day or swing trading is to identify a trend in the market. This could be an uptrend, a downtrend, or a sideways trend.

Setting entry and exit points: Once the trend has been identified, the trader will set entry and exit points for their trades. These points could be based on technical analysis, such as support and resistance levels or chart patterns, or they could be based on fundamental analysis, such as economic data or company news.

Entering a trade: When the market reaches the entry point, the trader will place a buy or sell order, depending on the direction of the trend.

Monitoring the trade: The trader will then monitor the trade, using stop-loss orders to limit potential losses and taking profits at the predetermined exit point.

Exiting the trade: When the market reaches the exit point, the trader will close the position and either take profits or cut losses, depending on the performance of the trade.

Summary

In the dominion of investing, growth and value investing stand out as two paths that lead to potential investment opportunities. Growth investing is a daring and audacious option, well-suited for investors with a long-term outlook and a willingness to take on higher risks. This investment approach offers the promise of higher returns, but it requires astute attention to detail and a willingness to weather market turbulence. In contrast, value investing is a more contemplative and strategic approach that involves seeking out undervalued companies and patiently waiting for the market to recognize their true worth.

Regardless of which path one chooses, it is essential to evaluate financial goals, risk tolerance, and time horizon carefully. Ultimately, successful investing requires a sound understanding of the investment landscape, a clear-eyed assessment of one's strengths and limitations, and the courage to make informed decisions with conviction.

Chapter 4

Investing Rules

Investing rules are like guiding stars in a dark sky, illuminating the path to financial success. They provide structure, discipline, and a framework for making smart investment decisions. At their core, investing rules are about managing risk and maximizing returns. They remind us to stay focused on our goals, avoid impulsive decisions, and remain patient in the face of market volatility.

Invest only what you can afford to lose: It's important to remember that investing carries inherent risks, and you should only invest an amount that you are comfortable potentially losing, especially in high-risk instruments.

Preserve Your Earnings: After securing a profit, it is prudent to withdraw your initial investment or, at the very least, a portion thereof, particularly from high-risk ventures. Consequently, the paramount objective ought to be the complete extraction of your initial investment, allowing you to reinvest and generate returns solely on capital gains.

Monitor liquidity: It's important to ensure that you have access to funds when you need them. Investing in assets that are difficult to sell quickly or require a long-term commitment can be risky if unexpected financial needs arise.

Be wary about borrowing to invest: The temptation to borrow funds to invest is always present, but the risks of leveraging should not be overlooked. If the investment value plummets, you could end up owing more than the borrowed amount, a devastating consequence.

Have a contingency plan: It's important to have a contingency plan in case unexpected events such as job loss or medical emergencies occur. This might involve having an emergency fund or considering insurance options.

Invest in what you understand: It's important to invest in assets that you understand and are familiar with. Investing in complex financial instruments that you don't fully comprehend can be risky and lead to losses.

Understand the risks of different types of investments: Different types of investments carry different levels of risk. It's important to understand the risks associated with each type of investment before you decide to invest in it.

Keep emotions in check: Emotions can cloud judgment and lead to impulsive investment decisions. It's important to stay rational and not let fear or greed drive your investment choices.

Diversify your portfolio: To mitigate risk and potentially reduce the impact of any one investment, spread your investments across a range of asset classes. This diversification approach can help you to safeguard your portfolio from market volatility.

Keep an eye on fees: Investment fees, such as management fees and trading costs, can eat into your returns. Be sure to consider the fees associated with different investments and choose ones that offer a good balance of risk and return.

Consider tax implications: Taxes can have a significant impact on investment returns, so it's important to consider the tax implications of your investment decisions. This might involve consulting with a tax professional or considering tax-efficient investment vehicles such as retirement accounts.

Avoid investing based on rumors or hype: Investing based on rumors or hype can lead to impulsive decisions and potential losses. It's important to do your own research and make informed investment decisions based on reliable information.

Have a long-term perspective: Investment success often requires patience. Instead of trying to time the market or make quick profits, consider adopting a long-term perspective and holding onto investments for the long haul.

Regularly review your investments: It's important to regularly review your investments to ensure that they are still aligned with your financial goals and risk tolerance. This might involve rebalancing your portfolio to ensure that you are diversified and making any necessary adjustments to your investments.

Don't be afraid to seek professional advice: If you are new to investing or uncertain about how to best achieve your financial goals, it can be helpful to seek the advice of a financial professional. They can help you to create a customized investment plan and provide guidance on making informed investment decisions.

Stay informed: Staying informed about economic and market trends can help you to make efficient investment decisions. This might involve reading financial news, studying market trends, or consulting with a financial professional.

Stay disciplined: Successful investing requires discipline and sticking to your investment plan even during market volatility or economic uncertainty. Avoid making impulsive decisions based on short-term market movements and stay focused on your long-term goals.

Summary

By forging a path that is focused on the long-term, staying well-informed, and creating a comprehensive financial plan, investors can navigate the often-treacherous waters of the investing world and increase their chances of success.

In conclusion, one truth remains steadfast, investing is a potent instrument for creating wealth, but it must be approached with wisdom and prudence. By adhering to these essential investment principles, you can mitigate the inherent risks of investing and amplify your prospects for prosperity.

Part II

Understanding Financial Markets

Chapter 5

What are Financial Markets?

Financial markets serve as the beating heart of the global economy, providing a platform for the exchange of resources between savers and borrowers. These dynamic and complex systems allow investors to buy and sell a range of financial instruments, including stocks, bonds, currencies, and commodities, enabling capital to flow from those who have surplus resources to those who need them.

Primary Markets: One of the most significant functions of financial markets is the allocation of capital to its most productive uses. This is achieved through the issuance of securities in primary markets. In primary markets, companies and governments raise capital by issuing stocks, bonds, and other securities to investors. These new securities provide a means for investors to channel their capital to promising projects and enterprises that have the potential to generate high returns. In doing so, primary markets contribute to the expansion of businesses and industries, creating jobs and driving economic growth.

The process of issuing securities in primary markets is often complex and time-consuming, involving an assortment of legal and regulatory requirements. Companies must divulge detailed reports about their operations, financial performance, and future prospects to potential investors, enabling them to make informed decisions about whether to invest. This process helps to build trust between investors and companies, promoting transparency and accountability in the financial system.

Secondary Markets: Secondary markets provide a platform for the trading of securities that have already been issued. In secondary markets, investors can buy and sell securities among themselves, rather than purchasing them directly from the issuer. This creates a more liquid market, where investors can easily enter and exit positions in response to changing market conditions. This liquidity can be vital for investors who need to quickly convert their holdings into cash.

Financial markets are not limited to the buying and selling of stocks and bonds. They also include currency markets, where traders buy and sell different currencies in response to global economic conditions. Commodities markets, such as those for oil, gold, and agricultural products, allow investors to hedge against price volatility and speculate on future market trends. These markets are highly interconnected, and movements in one market can have a significant impact on others.

Governments and regulatory bodies play a critical role in ensuring that financial markets function smoothly and efficiently. Through regulatory frameworks that promote transparency and protect investors from fraud and abuse, confidence is built among investors, promoting long-term stability.

In conclusion, financial markets play a pivotal role in the global economy and require ongoing attention and regulation to ensure their continued success.

Types of Financial Markets

The ever-evolving world of finance is home to a multitude of markets, each with its own unique characteristics and functions that collectively make up the intricate fabric of the global financial system. Financial markets serve different investment objectives and market participants.

Stock markets: these markets allow publicly traded companies to sell ownership stakes in the form of stocks to raise capital, while investors buy stocks to share in the profits and growth of the company.

Bond markets: these markets allow companies and governments to borrow money by issuing bonds, which are essentially loan agreements that pay a fixed rate of interest over a certain period of time. Investors buy bonds to lend money to the issuer in exchange for interest payments.

Commodity markets: these markets allow producers of raw materials to sell their products to buyers and hedge against price fluctuations, while investors can trade commodities to diversify their portfolios and profit from price changes.

Foreign exchange markets: these markets allow individuals and institutions to buy and sell currencies to facilitate international trade and investment.

Derivatives markets: these markets allow investors to speculate on the future price movements of financial instruments or to hedge against risk. Derivatives are financial instruments that are derived from an underlying asset, such as a stock or commodity.

Real estate markets: these markets allow the buying and selling of land, buildings, and other types of real property, which can be a valuable investment for individuals and institutions as the value of property can appreciate over time.

Money markets: these markets are a source of short-term financing for governments, financial institutions, and businesses, where short-term debt securities, such as Treasury bills and commercial paper, are traded.

Insurance markets: these markets allow individuals and institutions to protect themselves against financial losses due to accidents, illnesses, and other events.

Art markets: these markets allow the buying and selling of works of art, with primary markets involving the sale of newly created works and secondary markets involving the resale of previously owned works.

Agricultural markets: these markets allow farmers and other producers to sell their products to buyers and hedge against price fluctuations.

Energy markets: these markets allow producers to sell their products and investors to trade energy commodities as a way to diversify their portfolios and profit from price changes.

Cryptocurrency markets: these markets allow for the buying and selling of digital currencies, which can be used as a store of value, a means of exchange, and a unit of account.

Private equity markets: these markets involve the buying and selling of securities in privately held companies, which are not publicly traded on a stock exchange.

Venture capital markets: these markets involve the buying and selling of securities in early-stage companies that are seeking funding to grow and scale their businesses.

Credit markets: these markets allow lenders to sell their loans to investors, who can then collect the interest and principal payments from borrowers.

Crowdfunding markets: these markets allow individuals and institutions to invest in and lend to businesses and other organizations through online platforms.

Other specialized financial markets include the social impact market, artificial intelligence market, music market, and environmental market. These markets cater to a wide range of investment interests and goals, providing opportunities for investors to diversify their portfolios and achieve their financial objectives.

Summary

In the dominion of finance, markets serve as the lifeblood of the global economy, facilitating the flow of capital from those possessing surplus resources to those in need. Primary markets aid companies and governments in raising capital, while secondary markets offer a platform for trading previously issued securities.

Various types of financial markets exist, encompassing stock, bond, currency, commodity, and real estate markets. Governments and regulatory bodies hold a pivotal role in ensuring the seamless and efficient operation of financial markets. These markets are intricately interconnected, with fluctuations in one market substantially influencing others. Ultimately, financial markets are crucial for fostering growth and development across businesses and industries, generating employment, and propelling progress.

Chapter 6

How Financial Markets Work

The flow of funds in an economy is a carefully orchestrated dance, led by the grand conductor that is the financial market. Buyers and sellers, brokers and dealers, exchanges and over-the-counter (OTC) markets all move in harmony to facilitate the transfer of funds from savers to borrowers, and to provide a means for individuals and institutions to invest and earn returns on their savings.

- Financial markets operate through a network of buyers and sellers, brokers and dealers, and additionally exchanges and over-the-counter (OTC) markets.

- In an exchange, such as a stock exchange, buyers and sellers come together to trade securities through a central marketplace. In an OTC market, transactions are conducted directly between buyers and sellers without a central marketplace.

Key points to understand about how financial markets work:

- Financial markets facilitate the buying and selling of financial instruments: Financial markets provide individuals and institutions with a platform to buy and sell financial instruments, which are the backbone of the financial industry. These instruments include stocks, bonds, currencies, and commodities, and are essential for investors to diversify their portfolios and manage risk.

- Financial markets provide liquidity: Liquidity is the ease with which an asset can be bought or sold in the market. Financial markets provide investors with the liquidity they need to quickly buy or sell financial instruments, which can be crucial in times of market volatility or economic uncertainty.

- Financial markets can be organized or informal: Financial markets can be organized and regulated, such as the New York Stock Exchange, or they can be informal and unregulated, such as the foreign exchange market. Organized markets typically have rules and procedures in place to ensure fair and transparent trading, while informal markets may be more susceptible to fraud and manipulation.

- Financial markets can be physical or virtual: Whether it's a bustling stock exchange or an online brokerage, financial markets can be found in both physical and virtual forms.

- Financial markets can be local or global: Whether it's a local stock exchange or a global currency market, financial markets can be both local and global, with diverse participants and varying levels of efficiency.

- Financial markets are subject to regulation: Financial markets are often subject to regulation by government agencies, such as securities and exchange commissions and central banks. These regulators are responsible for ensuring fair and transparent trading, protecting investors from fraud and abuse, and maintaining the stability of the financial system.

- Financial markets can be volatile: Financial markets can experience periods of volatility, with sharp price movements and high levels of uncertainty. Volatility can be caused by a variety of factors, including economic shocks, political events, and changes in investor sentiment. While volatility can create opportunities for traders and investors, it can also lead to significant losses and risks.

- Financial markets are constantly evolving: Financial markets are constantly evolving as new financial instruments, technologies, and regulations emerge. This can lead to new opportunities for investors and intermediaries, but it can also create new risks and challenges that need to be addressed.

- Financial markets impact the economy: Financial markets play an important role in the broader economy by allocating capital to businesses and governments, facilitating investment and economic growth, and influencing the cost of capital for borrowers. Changes in financial markets can have a ripple effect throughout the economy, impacting employment, inflation, and overall economic activity.

Summary

Financial markets are an essential component of the economy, orchestrating the flow of funds from savers to borrowers and enabling individuals and institutions to invest and earn returns on their savings. They operate through a network of buyers and sellers, brokers and dealers, and exchanges and over-the-counter markets. Financial instruments such as stocks, bonds, currencies, and commodities are bought and sold in financial markets, which can be physical or virtual, organized or informal, global or local. Through countless transactions, financial markets play a crucial role in connecting investors and businesses and driving the flow of funds that fuel economic growth.

Chapter 7

Key Players in Financial Markets

The financial markets are an ensemble of actors, each with their own distinct part to play in the grand symphony of commerce. Among these key players are:

Investors: Investors are individuals or institutions that buy and sell financial instruments in order to earn a return on their investment or speculate on the future value of an asset. Investors can include retail investors, such as individual investors, and institutional investors, such as mutual funds and pension funds.

Issuers: Issuers are companies and governments that issue and sell securities, such as stocks and bonds, to raise capital. Issuers use the proceeds from the sale of securities to fund their operations and projects.

Intermediaries: Intermediaries, such as brokers and dealers, facilitate the buying and selling of financial instruments by connecting buyers and sellers and executing trades on behalf of their clients. Intermediaries often provide market information and other services to their clients.

Regulators: Regulators are government agencies that oversee and regulate financial markets to ensure fair and transparent trading and protect investors from fraud and abuse. Regulators can include central banks, securities and exchange commissions, and other government agencies.

Market makers: Market makers are firms or individuals that buy and sell financial instruments in order to facilitate trading and provide liquidity to the market. Market makers often hold inventory of securities and are willing to buy or sell at any time, regardless of the current market conditions.

Rating agencies: Rating agencies are firms that evaluate the creditworthiness of securities, such as bonds, and assign ratings based on the issuer's ability to make timely payments of interest and principal. Rating agencies provide investors with information about the risk of investing in a particular security.

Financial advisers: Financial advisers are professionals who provide advice and guidance to individuals and institutions on financial matters, such as investment strategies and asset allocation. Financial advisers can work for banks, investment firms, or as independent advisers.

Central banks: These institutions play a crucial role in financial markets by regulating the money supply, setting interest rates, and providing liquidity to financial institutions in times of crisis. Central banks also oversee the stability of the banking system and are responsible for maintaining the value of the currency.

Hedge funds: These investment funds typically cater to wealthy individuals and institutions and employ a range of sophisticated investment strategies to generate high returns. Hedge funds are known for their flexibility, agility, and ability to take on significant risk in pursuit of higher profits.

Pension funds: These funds manage the retirement savings of millions of individuals and invest in a wide range of assets, including stocks, bonds, and real estate. Pension funds typically have long-term investment horizons and seek to generate steady returns to fund the retirement benefits of their members.

Sovereign wealth funds: These funds are owned by governments and invest in a range of assets, including stocks, bonds, and real estate, on behalf of the country's citizens. Sovereign wealth funds are typically used to save excess revenue from natural resource exports or to diversify a country's foreign reserves.

Summary

The financial markets are a complex and intricate web of diverse players, each with their own distinct purpose and contribution. From investors seeking to earn a return on their investments, to issuers raising capital through the sale of securities, to regulators ensuring fair and transparent trading, the key players in financial markets are numerous and diverse.

Market makers provide liquidity and rating agencies evaluate creditworthiness, while financial advisers offer guidance and central banks regulate money supply and oversee stability. Hedge funds seek high returns through risk-taking, while pension funds aim to generate steady returns for retirement savings. Sovereign wealth funds invest on behalf of citizens and diversify foreign reserves. The symphony of commerce could not exist without the harmonious collaboration of these essential key players.

Part III

Investing in Specific Asset Classes

Chapter 8

Stock Market

The stock market is a domain where investors engage in the art of trading shares of publicly traded companies with the hope of yielding capital appreciation or dividend income. Through the strategic and calculated practice of buying low and selling high, investors stand to make substantial profits.

For instance, imagine an investor procuring 100 shares of a company's stock at $50 per share. If the company's stock price subsequently surges to $60 per share, the investor's profit would be a remarkable $1,000 (100 x $10). The investor may choose to sell their shares to reap these profits or keep them in the hopes of further price appreciation.

Investors typically purchase stocks through a brokerage account, and the value of the stock is dictated by the dynamics of supply and demand in the market. The value of a stock may fluctuate depending on various factors such as the company's financial performance, industry conditions, along with macroeconomic trends.

Investing in the stock market offers several benefits, such as the potential for high returns, especially if an investor selects well-performing companies. Some stocks pay dividends, which can serve as a source of income for the investor. Moreover, many investors opt for mutual funds or exchange-traded funds (ETFs) that offer professional management and diversification.

However, investing in the stock market comes with its fair share of risks. Market risk is an ever-present reality, whereby an investor's portfolio may appreciate or depreciate depending on market conditions. Company-specific risk is another factor to consider, as the financial performance and management of a company can significantly impact the performance of an individual stock.

Types of Stocks

Amidst the vastness of the stock market, various types of stocks flourish, each with their inimitable characteristics and offerings.

Common stock, the most rudimentary of all, represents ownership in a company. With common shares, shareholders hold voting rights and partake in the company's profits through dividends.

Preferred stock, on the other hand, is a type of stock that commands a higher priority claim on the company's assets and earnings than common stock. Holding preferred shares endows shareholders with the privilege of receiving dividends before those with common shares. Furthermore, preferred stock often features a fixed dividend rate, which provides greater stability to investors.

To further complicate matters, some companies issue different classes of stock, such as **Class A and Class**

B. These distinctions serve to allocate different voting rights or dividend claims to different classes of shareholders, depending on their level of investment.

Classification of Stocks

Stocks can be classified into various categories based on different criteria, such as growth potential, valuation, risk, market capitalization, sector, and geography. Understanding these classifications can help investors make informed decisions when selecting stocks that align with their investment objectives and risk tolerance.

Growth stocks are stocks of companies that are expected to grow at a faster rate than the overall market. These companies typically have high earnings growth potential, but may also be riskier due to their higher valuation.

Value stocks are stocks of companies that are undervalued by the market and are expected to have a higher return than the overall market. These companies may have lower growth potential, but may also be less risky due to their lower valuation.

Income stocks are stocks of companies that pay a high dividend yield and are often used by investors as a source of income. These companies may have lower growth potential, but may also be less risky due to their steady dividend payments.

Blue chip stocks are stocks of well-established companies with a strong track record of performance and stability. These companies are often leaders in their industry and are considered to be less risky than smaller or newer companies.

Penny stocks are stocks that trade for less than $1 per share and are often associated with small, risky companies. These stocks may have higher volatility and may be more difficult to buy and sell due to lower liquidity.

Cyclical stocks are stocks of companies that are sensitive to changes in the business cycle, such as consumer goods companies or industrial companies. These stocks tend to perform well during economic expansions and poorly during economic contractions.

Defensive stocks are stocks of companies that are less sensitive to changes in the business cycle, such as utilities or healthcare companies. These stocks tend to perform well during economic downturns and provide a degree of stability to a portfolio.

Microcap stocks are stocks of very small companies with market capitalizations (Number of outstanding shares x Current market price per share) of less than $300 million. These stocks may be riskier and more volatile than stocks of larger companies and may be more difficult to buy and sell due to lower liquidity.

Small cap stocks are stocks of small companies with market capitalizations between $300 million and $2 billion. These stocks may have higher growth potential, but may also be riskier due to their smaller size and lower liquidity.

Large cap stocks are stocks of large companies with market capitalizations of more than $10 billion. These stocks may be less risky and volatile than smaller stocks but may also have lower growth potential.

International stocks are stocks of companies that are based in foreign countries. Investing in international stocks can provide investors with diversification and the opportunity to benefit from economic growth in other countries, but it also carries additional risks, such as political and economic instability, currency volatility, and different regulatory environments.

Emerging market stocks are stocks of companies that are based in developing countries, such as Brazil, China, or India. These stocks can offer investors the opportunity to benefit from higher growth potential and economic development in emerging markets, but they also carry additional risks, such as political and economic instability, currency volatility, and higher default rates.

REITs, or real estate investment trusts, are companies that own and operate income-producing real estate, such as shopping malls, apartment buildings, or office buildings. REITs are required to distribute a significant portion of their income to shareholders in the form of dividends, making them a popular choice for income-oriented investors.

Stock market indices

A stock market index is a powerful statistical tool that tracks the performance of a group of stocks, providing a comprehensive snapshot of the market or a particular sector. By calculating the price changes of the stocks in the index and weighting them according to their market capitalization, the resulting index value is an accurate measure of the overall performance of the market or sector.

Stock market indices can be global or local, broad or narrow, and each has its own unique characteristics. Global indices often encompass a vast array of stocks from around the world, providing a broad representation of the market and a diversity of sectors. Local indices, on the other hand, tend to be more concentrated and less diverse, tracking the performance of stocks from a particular region or country.

Broad indices are designed to provide a comprehensive overview of the market, while narrow indices track the performance of a specific sector or industry. Ticker symbols are used to identify the index and track its performance in real-time, allowing investors and analysts to compare the performance of a particular stock or fund to the performance of a relevant index and gauge its relative performance.

In summary, stock market indices are a critical tool for investors and analysts to assess the performance of the stock market and individual stocks. By providing a statistical measure of the market or sector, stock market indices offer a valuable benchmark for investors to compare their own investments and make informed decisions.

Types of Stock Market Indices

S&P 500 is a broad-based index that tracks the performance of 500 large-cap stocks listed on the New York Stock Exchange and the NASDAQ. It is widely followed as a benchmark for the overall performance of the U.S. stock market and is often used as a benchmark for the performance of mutual funds and other investment products.

Dow Jones Industrial Average (DJIA) is a price-weighted index that tracks the performance of 30 blue-chip stocks listed on the New York Stock Exchange and the NASDAQ. It is often used as a benchmark for the overall performance of the U.S. stock market and is considered a barometer of the overall health of the economy.

NASDAQ Composite is a market-capitalization-weighted index that tracks the performance of all the stocks listed on the NASDAQ stock exchange. It is a broad-based index that covers a wide range of sectors and is often used as a benchmark for the performance of technology and internet-related stocks.

Russell 2000 is a market-capitalization-weighted index that tracks the performance of the 2,000 smallest publicly traded companies in the Russell 3000 Index. It is often used as a benchmark for the performance of small-cap stocks and is considered a good indicator of the overall health of the U.S. economy.

S&P/TSX Composite is a market-capitalization-weighted index that tracks the performance of the top 250 companies listed on the Toronto Stock Exchange. It is widely followed as a benchmark for the overall performance of the Canadian stock market and is often used as a benchmark for the performance of international funds.

MSCI Emerging Markets Index is a market-capitalization-weighted index that tracks the performance of emerging market stocks from around the world. It is a broad-based index that covers a wide range of sectors and is often used as a benchmark for the performance of emerging market funds.

MSCI World Index is a market-capitalization-weighted index that tracks the performance of developed market stocks from around the world. It is a broad-based index that covers a wide range of sectors and is often used as a benchmark for the performance of international funds.

Bloomberg Commodity Index is a price-weighted index that tracks the performance of 22 commodities, including energy, metals, and agricultural products. It is widely followed as a benchmark for the overall performance of the commodity market and is often used as a benchmark for the performance of commodity funds.

FTSE 100 is a market-capitalization-weighted index that tracks the performance of the 100 largest companies listed on the London Stock Exchange. It is widely followed as a benchmark for the overall performance of the U.K. stock market and is often used as a benchmark for the performance of international funds.

Nikkei 225 is a price-weighted index that tracks the performance of 225 blue-chip stocks listed on the Tokyo Stock Exchange. It is widely followed as a benchmark for the overall performance of the

Japanese stock market and is often used as a benchmark for the performance of international funds.

Hang Seng Index is a market-capitalization-weighted index that tracks the performance of the 50 largest companies listed on the Hong Kong Stock Exchange. It is widely followed as a benchmark for the overall performance of the Hong Kong stock market and is often used as a benchmark for the performance of international funds.

BSE Sensex is a market-capitalization-weighted index that tracks the performance of the top 30 companies listed on the Bombay Stock Exchange (BSE). The BSE Sensex is widely followed as a benchmark for the overall performance of the Indian stock market.

Nifty 50 is a market-capitalization-weighted index that tracks the performance of the top 50 companies listed on the National Stock Exchange of India. It is widely followed as a benchmark for the overall performance of the Indian stock market and is often used as a barometer for the performance of large-cap Indian stocks.

FTSE MIB is a market-capitalization-weighted index that tracks the performance of the 40 largest companies listed on the Italian stock exchange. It is widely followed as a benchmark for the overall performance of the Italian stock market and is often used as a benchmark for the performance of international funds investing in Italy.

DAX is a market-capitalization-weighted index that tracks the performance of the 30 largest and most actively traded companies on the Frankfurt Stock Exchange in Germany. It is widely followed as a benchmark for the overall performance of the German stock market and is often used as a benchmark for the performance of European funds.

CBOE Volatility Index (VIX), commonly known as the "**fear index**," serves as a measure of investor sentiment and market risk. It reflects the market's expectation of 30-day volatility and is calculated using the prices of options on the S&P 500 Index.

A high VIX value signifies high expected volatility, while a low VIX value indicates low expected volatility. Unlike traditional stock market indices, the VIX is not directly tied to the performance of a group of stocks but rather to the market's expectation of future volatility. The VIX is widely used by investors and traders as a barometer of market risk and to make informed decisions about their stock positions based on whether the VIX is indicating an uptrend, downtrend, or correction.

- In Figure 8.1, VIX reflects a surge in market volatility, indicating a correction (downward trend) in the stock market.

Figure 8.1: $VIX analysis on StockCharts.com

These are but a mere handful of the multitudinous stock market indices that exist, each possessing its own distinctive methodology and purpose. Whether you are a diligent individual investor navigating the constantly changing market, an experienced fund manager making informed investment decisions, or a perceptive financial analyst seeking to uncover underlying trends driving economic growth, developing a deep understanding of these indices' attributes and performance can provide valuable insights into the fluctuations of the stock market and the broader economy.

Stock market sectors

Stock market sectors are a methodical grouping of companies that operate in similar industries, imbued with the power to unveil industry-specific trends and performance. By categorizing stocks based on their sector or industry, investors and analysts are better equipped to make informed decisions and gain deeper insights into the intricate workings of the market.

Key points to consider about stock market sectors:

- **Classifying stocks**: The fundamental purpose of stock market sectors is to classify stocks according to industry or sector. This categorization allows investors and analysts to appraise the performance of a specific industry or sector and draw informed conclusions about investment decisions.

- **Business activities**: Stock market sectors are rooted in the business activities of the companies that they encompass. For instance, companies in the technology sector primarily develop and sell technology products and services, while companies in the healthcare sector specialize in healthcare products and services.

- **Broad or narrow sectors**: Stock market sectors can either be broad, spanning a range of industries, or narrow, focusing on a specific industry or sector. Broad sectors offer a panoramic view of the market, while narrow sectors provide a more in-depth understanding of a particular industry or sector.

- **Performance analysis**: Stock market sectors serve as a powerful analytical tool for assessing industry or sector performance. Investors and analysts often compare the performance of a specific stock or fund to the performance of a relevant sector to gain insight into its relative performance.

- **Diverse industries**: Stock market sectors cover a wide array of industries, ranging from healthcare, technology, and finance to energy, consumer goods, and more. With each industry characterized by unique nuances and dynamics, sector analysis provides a valuable means of identifying trends and opportunities that may be invisible at a broader market level.

- **Uncovering market trends**: The performance of stock market sectors can also provide a valuable window into broader market trends and shifts. For example, the relative performance of sectors such as technology and healthcare can offer insights into broader demographic, social, and technological changes that are shaping the economy and society.

- **Making informed decisions**: The ability to analyze the performance of a specific industry or sector through sector analysis enables investors and analysts to make informed decisions about stock investments. By understanding the unique characteristics of a sector and its constituents, investors can better assess risks and opportunities and identify companies that align with their investment goals.

Examples of stock market sectors and subsectors:

Technology: In this sector, companies that develop and sell technology products and services are grouped together. The technology sector includes subsectors such as software, hardware, and telecommunications, each with its unique nuances and dynamics.

> **Examples:** Apple, Microsoft, Alphabet Inc. (Google), Meta, Intel

Communication Services: Companies that facilitate communication and information exchange. This sector includes industries such as media, telecommunications, and entertainment, among others.

> **Examples:** AT&T Inc., Twitter Inc., Electronic Arts Inc., Comcast Corporation, Verizon Communications Inc.

Healthcare: Companies that develop and sell healthcare products and services are grouped under this sector. The healthcare sector encompasses subsectors such as pharmaceuticals, medical devices, and healthcare services, each with its own challenges and opportunities.

> **Examples:** Pfizer Inc., Johnson & Johnson, Roche Holding AG, Merck & Co., Inc., Novartis International AG

Consumer Staples: This sector comprises companies that produce and sell essential goods and services that are consumed on a regular basis. Subsectors within this sector include food and beverage, household products, and personal care products, each with its own market trends and shifts.

Examples: The Coca-Cola Company, Procter & Gamble Co., Nestle SA, PepsiCo, Inc., Unilever PLC

Consumer Discretionary: The consumer discretionary sector includes companies that produce and sell non-essential goods and services that are consumed on a discretionary basis. The subsectors within this sector, such as retail, media, and leisure, offer unique insights into the broader social and cultural trends that shape consumer behavior.

Examples: Amazon.com, Inc., Walt Disney Company, Nike, Inc., Netflix, Inc., Ford Motor Company

Energy: The energy sector includes companies that produce and sell energy-related products and services. The subsectors within this sector, such as oil and gas, renewable energy, and power, are subject to unique geopolitical, environmental, and technological forces.

Examples: ExxonMobil Corporation, Royal Dutch Shell plc, BP plc, Chevron Corporation, Eni S.p.A.

Financials: Companies that provide financial services are grouped under this sector. The subsectors within this sector, such as banking, insurance, and investment management, offer unique insights into the broader economic and regulatory trends that shape the financial industry.

Examples: JPMorgan Chase & Co., Bank of America Corporation, Wells Fargo & Company, Visa Inc., Goldman Sachs Group, Inc.

Industrials: The industrials sector includes companies that produce and sell industrial products and services. The subsectors within this sector, such as aerospace and defense, construction and engineering, and transportation, offer unique insights into the broader technological and infrastructural trends that shape industrial development.

Examples: General Electric Company, Caterpillar Inc., Boeing Company, 3M Company, Siemens AG

Materials: Companies that produce and sell raw materials are grouped under this sector. The subsectors within this sector, such as chemicals, metals and mining, and forestry and paper, are subject to unique environmental, geopolitical, and economic forces.

Examples: BHP Group Limited, Rio Tinto Group, DuPont de Nemours, Inc., The Dow Chemical Company, Vale S.A.

Real Estate: Companies that own, develop, and manage real estate properties are grouped under this sector. The subsectors within this sector, such as residential, commercial, and industrial properties, offer unique insights into the broader demographic, urbanization, and regulatory trends that shape real estate development.

Examples: Simon Property Group, Inc., Prologis, Inc., Public Storage, Equinix, Inc., American Tower Corporation

Utilities: The utilities sector includes companies that produce and distribute utility services. The subsectors within this sector, such as electricity, gas, and water utilities, offer unique insights into the broader environmental, regulatory, and technological trends that shape utility services.

Examples: NextEra Energy, Inc., Duke Energy Corporation, Dominion Energy, Inc., National Grid plc, Enel S.p.A.

Essentially, stock market sectors serve as a critical compass for investors and analysts, skillfully categorizing stocks according to their industry or sector, revealing profound insights and informed decision-making. These sectors span a spectrum of breadth, from the vast expanse of technology, healthcare, consumer goods, to the compelling world of energy. Meticulously scrutinizing the performance of these sectors can reveal a treasure trove of knowledge, uncovering invaluable market trends and shifts, while the subsectors within each industry offer a nuanced understanding of unique challenges and opportunities. Sector analysis ultimately empowers investors to make shrewd decisions, identifying companies that align with their investment objectives and deftly assessing the risks and opportunities that lie ahead.

How to choose stocks

In the pursuit of selecting stocks, it is vital to explore a plethora of elements, from the financial well-being of the company and its innovative prowess to market trends, competitive edge, growth potential, valuation, industry landscape, competitors, and portfolio supervision. By diving deep into these factors and conducting meticulous research, you can make astute investment decisions that align with your investment aspirations and risk appetite.

Key points to remember when picking stocks:

- **Start with a Plan**: Before you start choosing stocks, it is essential to have a well-defined investment plan. Determine your investment goals, time horizon, and risk tolerance. Based on your goals, decide on the type of stocks you want to invest in, such as growth stocks, value stocks, dividend stocks, or a combination of these.

- **Consider Macroeconomic Factors**: Before analyzing specific companies and industries, it is important to consider broader macroeconomic factors that may impact the stock market, such as interest rates, inflation, and geopolitical events. These factors can have a significant impact on the overall market and individual stocks, so it is important to stay informed and adjust your investment strategy accordingly.

- **Check Market calendar events regularly**: The market calendar includes a range of events that can shake stock prices, such as earnings releases, economic data, employment data, interest rate changes and central bank meetings. When analyzing stocks, it is imperative to consider market calendar events and how they may influence a company's stock price.

Example:
https://www.forexfactory.com/calendar
On the top menu bar, click on Calendar, then the yellow folder under the 'Detail' column - Review the event section: "Why Traders Care".

Table 8.1 categorizes the various factors that impact the market. The factors are organized based on their respective categories, highlighting the different economic, political, industry-specific, and external factors that can influence the market.

Category	Factors	Market Impact
Economic	Interest Rates	Direct
	Inflation	Direct
	GDP	Direct
	Consumer Spending	Direct
	Business Investment	Direct
	Unemployment	Inverse
	Trade Deficits	Inverse
Political	Government Policies	Direct
	Elections	Indirect
	International Relations	Indirect
Industry-Specific	Supply and Demand	Direct
	Labor Market	Direct
	Technological Innovation	Direct
External Factors	Natural Disasters	Indirect
	Pandemics	Indirect
	Global Economic Conditions	Indirect
	Geopolitical Tensions	Indirect

Table 8.1: Classification of Market Impact

Market Impact	Impact Interpretation
Direct	Immediate and noticeable impact on the market.
Inverse	Opposite effect on the market.
Indirect	Less clear or delayed impact on the market.

Table 8.2: Legend for Table 8.1

Please note that this illustrative chart is not exhaustive, as countless other elements hold the potential to alter the market's trajectory. Additionally, certain factors may wield both direct and indirect influence over the market, depending on the prevailing circumstances.

- **Gauge Market Volatility and Sentiment**: Market volatility can be a key factor to consider when making investment decisions. A helpful tool for gauging volatility in the stock market is the $VIX on StockCharts.com (as outlined in the preceding section) which serves as an inverse measure of market volatility. A downward trend in the VIX can indicate an upward trend in the market, and vice versa.

  Investors can also monitor the Fear Index on: https://www.cnn.com/markets/fear-and-greed, to evaluate investor sentiment and risk levels, providing valuable context for buying or selling decisions.

Through careful analysis of market trends (uptrend, downtrend, sideways or correction), investors can glean priceless insights into the trajectory of the market and make informed decisions about their stock positions. Yet, one must remember that market direction is rooted in historical price movements and trend analysis, and must not be viewed as the sole arbiter of investment decisions.

- **Recognize market cycles:** Understanding market cycles is an essential art for investors seeking to unlock the full potential of their investments. These cycles represent the rhythmic movement of the stock market, shaped by economic conditions, business cycles, and investor sentiment. As each market sector, such as technology, energy, consumer goods, and financial services, possesses unique dynamics, distinct cycles arise in each.

   For instance, technology stocks, a sector known for its sensitivity to economic conditions. Relying heavily on innovation and new product development, technology stocks can suffer during a recession or economic downturn as consumers cut back on discretionary spending. Conversely, consumer staples such as food and household goods are defensive sectors, providing essential goods and services that tend to perform well during economic hardship.

   By analyzing market cycles across various sectors, investors can make informed decisions regarding portfolio allocation. Historical market data, investor sentiment, and macroeconomic indicators can help identify potential opportunities and risks, accounting for current economic conditions and industry trends.

Investors can explore these cycles on platforms such as StockCharts.com (Under **Sector Summary and Industry Summary**) offering a window into the complexity and splendour of the market.

- **Scrutinize regulatory risks** loom large in the investment world, and they must be considered in full. Changes in government policies, regulations, or laws may cause operational and financial hurdles, impacting the stock price and investor's bottom line.

- **Identify High-Impact Stocks**: Track stocks with significant volume changes using https://finance.yahoo.com/gainers or similar websites, which can reveal promising opportunities or potential pitfalls.

- **Screen for stocks**: By screening stocks, we gaze through a prism of criteria that filter out the worthy few. Screening for stocks is the discerning compass that guides investors in pinpointing promising investment opportunities from a vast and ever-expanding universe of available stocks. Through the artful application of specific criteria, one can refine their search, honing in on those rare gems that hold the potential for growth.

Harness the potential of stock screening tools available on financial platforms like *Yahoo Finance, Finviz, or TradingView* to elevate your investment strategy. These invaluable tools enable you to input your desired criteria, filtering out irrelevant stocks and providing a list of stocks that meet your requirements.

Table 8.3 showcases some of the key screening criteria that investors can employ to identify promising stocks. With a minimum stock price of $20, and a high trading volume (above 1.1) assures sufficient institutional investor interest, along with a certain level of stability and liquidity. Additionally, a minimum market cap of $2 billion provides an indication of the company's overall size and importance in the market.

By focusing on companies that have experienced substantial sales growth, investors can identify potential market leaders. Examining the company's annual sales growth enables investors to compare overall performance, making informed decisions on potential investments.

Ticker Symbol	Stock Price	Volume	Sales Growth Last 3 quarters	Annual Sales Growth	Market Capitalization	Relative Volume
ABC	$25.75	8.2 million	30%	27%	$4.1 billion	1.8
XYZ	$22.10	5.5 million	28%	33%	$2.3 billion	2.0
DEF	$21.20	6.8 million	35%	29%	$3.7 billion	1.6
GHI	$24.90	7 million	26%	34%	$3.2 billion	1.9
JKL	$28.30	5.2 million	40%	26%	$2.1 billion	1.5

Table 8.3: Stock Screening Example

Low-priced stocks may be tempting to investors, but it is crucial to remember that they often carry high risks due to their low liquidity. Investing in stocks that are priced at $15 or more can help mitigate some of these risks.

- **Assess institutional interest**: In the grand theater of financial markets, a unique ensemble of powerful players graces the stage: the mighty institutions. These behemoths of the financial world wield unparalleled influence, their every move casting ripples that reverberate through the very fabric of the stock market. The symphony of institutional interest, a harmonious blend of pension funds, mutual funds, and hedge funds, orchestrates the momentum and direction of the stocks they choose to embrace.

These institutions, like celestial bodies, exert a gravitational pull on the stocks they favor, drawing the attention of individual investors and elevating valuations. Their vast resources and research capabilities offer them insights and foresight that can sway the tides of the market, inspiring confidence and shaping trends.

For those who wish to peer into the terrains of institutional investments, a myriad of resources lay at their fingertips:

WhaleWisdom: This treasure trove of data delves into the depths of institutional and hedge fund investment activities. By tracking 13F, 13D, and 13G filings, WhaleWisdom unveils the inscrutable world of institutional investments, shedding light on the stocks that stir the interest of these influential players. https://whalewisdom.com

Holdings Channel: Holdings Channel is an invaluable resource for those seeking information on institutional holdings. The platform consolidates 13F filings, offering detailed information on the stock holdings of various institutions. https://www.holdingschannel.com

MarketSmith by IBD: MarketSmith is a premium stock research platform developed by Investor's Business Daily. It provides users with comprehensive stock charts, screening

tools, and investment research, as well as data on institutional ownership.
https://www.marketsmith.com

Before placing a trade order, one must be mindful of the dual pillars of astute analysis: the Fundamental and Technical. These guiding beacons illuminate the path to informed decision-making, ensuring that the investor traverses the complex financial landscape with a discerning eye and unwavering confidence.

- **Fundamental Analysis,** delves deep into the very essence of a company, examining its financial health and intrinsic value. By scrutinizing elements such as revenue growth, earnings, balance sheets, and industry position, the investor gains invaluable insights into the company's stability and long-term prospects. The careful assessment of these critical factors forms the cornerstone of a sound investment strategy.

- **Technical Analysis,** represents the intricate dance of market forces, capturing the ebb and flow of stock prices as they weave their patterns upon the tapestry of time. This approach embraces the art of charting, analyzing historical price movements, and identifying trends to predict future trajectories. As the investor traces the delicate footprints of price and volume, they gain a profound understanding of the market's temperament, harnessing its rhythms to make well-timed and informed investment decisions.

Chapter 18 and 19 offers an in-depth examination of Fundamental and Technical Analysis, respectively.

Common Pitfalls in Stock Picking

The perplexing demesne of stock market investing, where fortunes sway in a delicate balance, is a journey laden with potential perils and unforeseen vicissitudes. As the allure of wealth beckons, the risks lurk in the shadows, poised to ensnare the unsuspecting, from seasoned maestros to fledgling entrants.

A prevalent pitfall ensconcing investors lies in the tumultuous embrace of emotions, where fear, greed, and panic cloud astute judgment, giving birth to impetuous and ill-conceived decisions. Succumbing to the siren call of investing beyond one's means or prematurely fleeing a plummeting market may result in forfeiting potential gains or cementing losses that patience could have circumvented.

Moreover, the folly of neglecting ample research is akin to gambling in the dark. Entrusting one's fortune to the superficial allure of glossy advertisements or striking earnings reports can culminate in calamity. A methodical excavation of financial records, industry trajectories, and competitive landscapes is paramount for judicious decision-making.

A crucial lesson for investors is to resist the tantalizing temptation of market timing. The capricious nature of the future defies prediction, and attempting to divine its course may yield missed opportunities or reckless gambles. Instead, crafting a steadfast long-term investment strategy, with periodic fine-tuning, serves as a more sagacious approach.

Investors must also tread carefully when treading the path of the masses. The stock market, susceptible to the whims of collective psychology, can generate ebullient bubbles or precipitous crashes. Solely mirroring the actions or beliefs of others, bereft of independent scrutiny, is a perilous endeavor.

Conclusively, astute investors must master the art of risk management. While the market's exhilaration can be intoxicating, every investment carries an inherent element of risk. Employing diversification, implementing stop-loss orders, and maintaining equanimity amidst market turbulence help mitigate these hazards. After all, triumph in the stock market lies not in evading risk but in skillfully navigating its treacherous waters.

Legendary Stock-Picking Strategies

Warren Buffett and his investment in Coca-Cola: In the early 1980s, Coca-Cola's stock was not performing well, and many investors were avoiding it. However, Buffett recognized the enduring popularity and value of the Coca-Cola brand and invested heavily in the company. This decision proved to be a sagacious one, as Coca-Cola's stock soared in the following years and has remained a profitable investment to this day.

Peter Lynch, a legendary investor who managed the Fidelity Magellan Fund from 1977 to

1990: Lynch believed in the power of "investing in what you know" and encouraged investors to look for investment opportunities in their everyday lives. One example he gave was his investment in Hanes, the well-known underwear brand. Lynch noticed that Hanes was a popular brand among his friends and family, and he recognized the company's potential for growth. He invested in Hanes and saw significant returns on his investment.

Apple's rise to dominance is often cited as a textbook example of picking a winning stock. In the early 2000s, Apple was seen as a niche player in the computer industry, with a loyal but relatively small customer base. However, with the launch of the iPod, iPhone, and iPad, Apple's stock soared, and the company became one of the most valuable in the world. The lesson here is that sometimes, investing in a company with a vision and a strong track record of innovation can pay off in a big way.

In the early 2000s, Netflix was a relatively unknown company that offered DVD rentals through the mail. However, the company's founder, Reed Hastings, recognized the shift in consumer behavior towards online streaming and began to pivot the company towards this new market. Despite skepticism from many investors and analysts, Hastings invested heavily in this new strategy and eventually phased out the DVD rental business entirely. This proved to be a shrewd decision, as Netflix's stock has since soared, and the company has become one of the biggest players in the entertainment industry. The lesson here is that sometimes, investing in a company with a bold vision and a willingness to adapt can lead to significant long-term gains.

These anecdotes demonstrate that successful stock picking requires a combination of research, intuition, and a willingness to think outside the box. By studying the successes of legendary investors and innovative companies, investors can gain valuable insights into what it takes to identify and invest in winning stocks.

Summary

Investing in the stock market is a nuanced art, where every move must be executed with precision and a deep understanding of the market's rhythm. Successful investors know the importance of diversification, spreading their assets across a range of securities to minimize risk. Maintaining a long-term perspective is also key, recognizing that investing is a journey with inevitable highs and lows. With steadfast commitment to your investment goals, diligence, and patience, you can confidently navigate the unpredictable tides of the market.

Amidst the excitement of investing, it is vital to remember that every investment carries some degree of risk. Effective risk management involves setting stop-loss orders, keeping a level head during market downturns, and being mindful of the risks and rewards associated with each investment decision. With discipline and a well-thought-out strategy, investors can execute a graceful and profitable dance in the stock market.

Chapter 9

Bond Market

The practice of bond market investing involves the trade of debt securities, issued by governments, municipalities, and companies. Akin to a loan, bond investors extend funds to the issuer and receive regular interest payments and the repayment of principal upon the bond's maturity.

For instance, imagine acquiring a bond with a face value of $1,000, a 5% annual interest rate, and a 10-year term. With this, the investor will receive yearly interest payments of $50 (5% x $1,000) and recoup the principal when the bond reaches maturity. However, the bond's risk level and interest rate depend on the issuer's creditworthiness and the bond term.

How the bond market works is relatively straightforward. Investors purchase bonds through brokerage accounts, and the bond's value is based on supply and demand. The bond's price may rise or fall based on several factors, including interest rates, credit ratings, and the financial health of the issuer.

There are several advantages to investing in bonds. They provide a reliable source of income through regular interest payments. Bonds can help diversify an investment portfolio as they tend to have a low correlation with stocks. Moreover, investors may opt for bond mutual funds or exchange-traded funds (ETFs) that offer professional management and diversification.

Nonetheless, bond investing carries certain risks. Interest rate risk is one such risk, as changes in interest rates can impact the bond's value. If interest rates rise, the value of an existing bond may decline. Credit risk is another concern as the issuer may fail to make payments, resulting in a loss of principal for the investor. Finally, liquidity risk is present in the bond market, where bonds may be less liquid than other investments, making it harder to purchase or sell them as needed.

Types of bonds

A diverse world of bonds looms, each with unique traits and rates. Corporate, municipal, and treasury, to name a few, offer varying levels of risk to ensue. From emerging markets to structured finance, and everything in between, investors have many options to glean. Whether seeking safety or yield, bonds can provide a stable financial stream.

Corporate bonds, are debt securities issued by companies to raise capital. They are typically issued with a fixed interest rate and a set maturity date, at which point the company must pay back the principal amount of the bond. Corporate bonds can be issued by companies of all sizes, from large, well-established firms to smaller, riskier companies.

Example: Apple Corporate Bond

Municipal bonds, also known as Munis, are debt securities issued by local or state governments to finance public projects, such as infrastructure or schools. They are typically issued with a fixed interest rate and a set maturity date, at which point the government must pay back the principal amount of the bond. Municipal bonds are generally considered to be lower risk than corporate bonds, as they are backed by the creditworthiness of the issuing government.

Example: New York City Municipal Bond

Treasury bonds, are debt securities issued by the U.S. government to finance its operations. They are typically issued with a fixed interest rate and a set maturity date, at which point the government must pay back the principal amount of the bond. Treasury bonds are generally considered to be the safest type of bond, as they are backed by the full faith and credit of the U.S. government.

Example: 10-year US Treasury Bond

Emerging market, bonds are debt securities issued by entities in developing countries, such as Brazil, China, or India. They can be classified by the type of issuer, such as sovereign bonds (issued by governments) or corporate bonds (issued by companies), or by the currency in which they are denominated, such as U.S. dollar-denominated bonds or local currency-denominated bonds. Emerging market bonds can offer investors the opportunity to benefit from higher yields and economic growth in developing countries, but they also carry additional risks, such as currency volatility, political and economic instability, and higher default rates.

Example: Brazil Sovereign Bond

Agency bonds, are debt securities issued by government-sponsored agencies, such as Fannie Mae or Freddie Mac. They are typically issued with a fixed interest rate and a set maturity date, at which point the agency must pay back the principal amount of the bond. Agency bonds are generally considered to be lower risk than corporate bonds, as they are backed by the creditworthiness of the issuing agency.

Example: Fannie Mae Agency Bond

Floating rate bonds, also known as variable rate bonds, are debt securities with a variable interest rate that is tied to a benchmark rate, such as the London Interbank Offered Rate (LIBOR). The interest rate on floating rate bonds adjusts periodically based on changes in the benchmark rate, which can provide protection against rising interest rates.

Example: JPMorgan Floating Rate Bond

Zero coupon bonds, also known as strip bonds, are debt securities that do not pay periodic interest payments. Instead, they are issued at a discount to their face value and mature at their face value, at which point the issuer must pay back the principal amount of the bond. Zero coupon bonds can be issued by any type of issuer, including corporations, governments, and agencies.

Example: US Treasury Strip Bond

High yield bonds, also known as junk bonds, are debt securities issued by companies with lower credit ratings. They are considered to be higher risk than investment grade bonds and are typically issued with higher interest rates to compensate for the added risk.

Example: General Electric Junk Bond

Convertible bonds, are debt securities that can be converted into equity at the holder's discretion. They are typically issued by companies that want to raise capital but also want to retain the option to issue equity in the future. Convertible bonds can provide investors with both income and the potential for capital appreciation if the company's stock price increases.

Example: Tesla Convertible Bond

Callable bonds, are debt securities that can be redeemed by the issuer before their maturity date. They are typically issued with a call provision that allows the issuer to redeem the bonds at a predetermined price, which can provide investors with an opportunity to sell the bonds back to the issuer before the maturity date.

Example: Goldman Sachs Callable Bond

Inflation-linked bonds, also known as inflation-protected bonds, are debt securities that are issued with an interest rate that is tied to an inflation index, such as the consumer price index (CPI). The interest rate on inflation-linked bonds adjusts periodically based on changes in the inflation index, which can provide protection against rising inflation.

Example: US Treasury Inflation-Protected Security (TIPS)

Asset-backed bonds, are debt securities that are backed by a specific pool of assets, such as mortgages, car loans, or credit card receivables. The value of the assets is used to secure the bond and can provide investors with a level of protection in the event that the issuer defaults on the bond.

Example: Ford Asset-Backed Bond

Municipal revenue bonds, are debt securities issued by local or state governments to finance specific projects, such as schools, hospitals, or infrastructure. They are typically backed by the revenue generated by the project, such as tolls or user fees, rather than the full faith and credit of the issuing government.

Example: Texas Municipal Revenue Bond

Structured finance bonds, are complex debt securities that are created by pooling and trancing various types of assets, such as mortgages or credit card receivables. They can be issued by a variety of entities, including banks, investment firms, and insurance companies.

Example: Lehman Brothers Structured Finance Bond

Corporate floating rate notes, are short-term debt securities with a variable interest rate that is tied to a benchmark rate, such as the London Interbank Offered Rate (LIBOR). They are issued by companies to raise capital and typically have a maturity date of one to three years.

> **Example**: Google Corporate Floating Rate Note

Asset-backed commercial paper, is a type of short-term debt security that is backed by a specific pool of assets, such as mortgages or credit card receivables. It is typically issued by financial institutions or other companies to raise short-term capital and has a maturity date of typically less than one year.

> **Example**: JPMorgan Asset-Backed Commercial Paper

Bond funds, are investment vehicles that invest in a diversified portfolio of bonds. They can be classified by the type of bonds they invest in, such as corporate bond funds or municipal bond funds, or by the duration of the bonds in the portfolio, such as short-term bond funds or long-term bond funds. Bond funds can provide investors with diversification and professional management, but they also carry additional risks, such as the risk of default or interest rate changes.

> **Example**: Vanguard Total Bond Market Index Fund

Bond market indices

The world of bonds is vast, intricate, and often daunting to the uninitiated. Bond market indices provide a glimpse into this world, offering a window into the performance of various segments of the bond market. These indices are benchmarks against which investors can measure their portfolios and analyze the performance of the underlying investments.

Bloomberg Barclays US Aggregate Bond Index: This Index is a widely-followed benchmark that tracks the performance of the U.S. investment grade bond market. It includes a broad range of bond types, such as Treasuries, corporate bonds, and mortgage-backed securities.

Bloomberg Barclays US Corporate Bond Index: This Index tracks the performance of the U.S. corporate bond market. It includes investment grade bonds issued by U.S. corporations.

Bloomberg Barclays US Treasury Bond Index: This Index tracks the performance of the U.S. Treasury bond market. It includes bonds issued by the U.S. government.

Bloomberg Barclays Municipal Bond Index: This Index tracks the performance of the U.S. municipal bond market. It includes bonds issued by local and state governments.

Bloomberg Barclays Global Aggregate Bond Index: This Index is a benchmark that tracks the performance of the global bond market. It includes a broad range of bond types, such as government bonds, corporate bonds, and mortgage-backed securities, and is denominated in multiple currencies.

JPMorgan Emerging Markets Bond Index: This Index tracks the performance of the emerging markets bond market. It includes bonds issued by governments and corporations in developing countries.

S&P/BGCantor US Treasury Bond Index: This Index tracks the performance of the U.S. Treasury bond market. It includes bonds issued by the U.S. government.

S&P/BGCantor US Corporate Bond Index: This Index tracks the performance of the U.S. corporate bond market. It includes investment grade bonds issued by U.S. corporations.

S&P/BGCantor US Mortgage-Backed Securities Index: This Index tracks the performance of the U.S. mortgage-backed securities market. It includes securities backed by residential and commercial mortgages.

S&P/BGCantor US High Yield Bond Index: This Index tracks the performance of the U.S. high yield bond market. It includes bonds that are rated below investment grade and may carry higher default risk.

S&P/BGCantor US Municipal Bond Index: This Index tracks the performance of the U.S. municipal bond market. It includes bonds issued by local and state governments.

FTSE Canada Universe Bond Index: This Index tracks the performance of the Canadian bond market. It includes a broad range of bond types, such as government bonds, corporate bonds, and mortgage-backed securities, and is denominated in Canadian dollars.

Citigroup World Government Bond Index: This Index tracks the performance of the global government bond market. It includes bonds issued by governments in developed and emerging markets and is denominated in multiple currencies.

Bloomberg Barclays Euro Aggregate Bond Index: This Index tracks the performance of the Eurozone bond market. It includes a broad range of bond types, such as government bonds, corporate bonds, and mortgage-backed securities, and is denominated in euros.

Bloomberg Barclays UK Gilt Index: This Index tracks the performance of the UK government bond market. It includes bonds issued by the UK government and is denominated in pounds sterling.

JPMorgan Asia Credit Index: This Index tracks the performance of the Asian credit market. It includes bonds issued by governments and corporations in Asia and is denominated in multiple currencies.

How to choose bonds

When venturing into the world of bonds, a mindful and thoughtful approach is paramount to forging a successful investment strategy that caters to your financial aspirations and risk appetite. Here are some vital considerations to keep in your heart and mind:

- **Identify your investment objectives**: Before you start choosing bonds, it's essential to determine what you hope to achieve with your investment. Your risk tolerance, return expectations, and investment horizon will help you identify the types of bonds that are most suitable for your needs.

- **Consider credit quality**: The credit quality of the bond issuer is a crucial factor to consider. Higher credit quality issuers, such as the U.S. government or highly rated corporations, may offer lower returns but carry lower default risk. Lower credit quality issuers, such as junk bonds or emerging market bonds, may offer higher returns but come with higher default risk.

- **Look at maturity**: The length of time until the bond reaches its final payment date, or maturity, is another important consideration. Longer maturity bonds may offer higher yields but may be more sensitive to interest rate changes and may be more volatile. Shorter maturity bonds may offer lower yields but may be less sensitive to interest rate changes and may be less volatile.

- **Examine yield**: The yield of a bond refers to the annual return an investor receives from the bond's interest payments. Higher yielding bonds may offer higher returns, but they may also carry higher risk, such as default risk or interest rate risk. Lower yielding bonds may offer lower returns, but they may also carry lower risk.

- **Consider tax implications**: The interest earned on most bonds is subject to federal income tax. Some bonds, such as municipal bonds, may be tax-exempt at the federal level, which can make them more attractive to investors in high tax brackets.

- **Look at liquidity**: The liquidity of a bond refers to how easily the bond can be bought or sold in the market. It's important to consider the liquidity of a bond when choosing which bonds to buy, as less liquid bonds may be more difficult to buy or sell in the market.

- **Research the bond issuer**: Before buying a bond, it's essential to research the bond issuer to understand the issuer's financial strength and creditworthiness. This can help you make informed decisions about the risk of default and the potential return of the bond.

- **Diversify your portfolio**: Diversifying your bond portfolio can help manage risk by spreading your investments across different types of bonds, issuers, and maturities. This can help reduce the impact of any one bond's performance on your overall portfolio.

- **Consult a financial advisor**: If you're uncertain about which bonds to buy or how to diversify your bond portfolio, it may be helpful to consult a financial advisor. A financial advisor can help you develop a bond investment strategy that aligns with your goals and risk tolerance.

Examples:

Sarah is seeking a safe investment to provide a steady stream of income. She chooses a 10-year US Treasury bond with a 3% coupon rate, which means she will receive annual interest payments of $30 for every $1,000 invested. The bond has a face value of $1,000, so she receives a total of $30 in annual interest and gets her $1,000 back when the bond matures in 10 years.

David is looking for a bond with a higher yield. He chooses a 5-year corporate bond issued by XYZ Company, which is a leading consumer goods manufacturer. The bond has a 6% coupon rate and is rated A by credit rating agencies, indicating a high level of creditworthiness. David buys the bond at a price of $1,000, so he receives annual interest payments of $60 and gets his $1,000 back when the bond matures in 5 years.

Useful resources to analyze bonds

Bloomberg.com: Bloomberg offers a vast amount of financial data and news, including bond market updates, bond yields, and credit ratings. It also provides in-depth analysis and research on individual bonds, as well as bond fund performance.

Morningstar.com: Morningstar is an investment research company that provides a range of financial data and research tools, including bond ratings, yields, and performance. Morningstar also offers a bond screener tool that allows investors to search for bonds based on specific criteria.

FINRA's Bond Section: The Financial Industry Regulatory Authority (FINRA) offers an extensive bond resource section that includes bond market data, educational materials, and tools for analyzing individual bonds.

TreasuryDirect.gov: TreasuryDirect is the official website of the US Treasury and provides information on US government bonds, including Treasury bills, notes, and bonds. The website offers a range of tools and resources for investors, including bond calculators and auction schedules.

FRED (Federal Reserve Economic Data): FRED is a vast database of economic data maintained by the Federal Reserve Bank of St. Louis. It includes bond market data, such as bond yields, interest rates, and inflation rates, as well as economic indicators and time-series data.

Avoiding Common Pitfalls

When picking bonds to invest in, there are mistakes and pitfalls that can leave investors in a bind. For those with a keen eye, the bond market can be a reliable source of income, but for the unwary, it can lead to financial ruin. The allure of high yields can be tempting, but investors must be careful not to fall into the traps.

One of the most common mistakes is to overlook the creditworthiness of the bond issuer. When a company or government agency issues a bond, they are effectively borrowing money from investors, and just like any borrower, they have a credit rating that reflects their ability to pay back the debt. Investors who neglect to assess the creditworthiness of the issuer may end up with a bond that is more likely to default, leaving them with little or no return on their investment.

Another common pitfall is chasing yield. High yields can be attractive, but they often come with a higher level of risk. Investors who focus solely on yield may end up investing in high-risk bonds that offer a higher yield but are more likely to default. It's important to consider the balance between risk and reward when selecting bonds.

Market timing is also a common mistake that can lead to poor returns. Attempting to time the market by buying and selling bonds based on market conditions is a risky strategy. Bond investors should instead focus on the long-term and invest in a diversified portfolio that includes a mix of bonds with different maturities and credit ratings.

Finally, investors should be wary of fees and expenses associated with bond investments. These costs can eat into returns and erode profits over time. It's essential to understand the fees associated with each bond investment and ensure they are reasonable before committing to the investment.

Summary

In the world of investing, bonds offer an avenue of stability, security, and income. However, selecting the right bonds to invest in requires careful consideration and attention to detail. By understanding the various types of bonds, their respective risks and rewards, and the importance of diversification, investors can create a well-balanced bond portfolio that meets their financial goals.

It's essential to avoid common mistakes, such as neglecting credit ratings, over-concentration in a single sector, and overlooking fees and expenses. With a thoughtful approach, investors can navigate the bond market with confidence and reap the benefits of this valuable asset class.

Chapter 10

Mutual Funds

A mutual fund, a magical union of multiple investors' resources, is an investment vehicle that acquires a diversified portfolio of securities, such as stocks, bonds, and other assets, to accomplish its ultimate objective. It aims to offer investors a platform for diversification of their investment portfolio and access to professional management at a modest cost.

For instance, the Vanguard 500 Index Fund, an exemplary mutual fund that tracks the performance of the S&P 500 Index, a yardstick index of 500 large-cap stocks listed on the New York Stock Exchange or NASDAQ. With the Vanguard 500 Index Fund, investors can experience an extensive range of large, publicly traded companies, all within a single fund. Vanguard, a notable investment management company, manages the fund, which is a cost-effective option for investors.

Investors purchase mutual fund shares, and the fund, in turn, invests the proceeds in a diverse range of assets, such as stocks, bonds, and other securities. The value of a mutual fund share is determined by the underlying assets' value in the fund's portfolio.

The benefits of mutual funds are multifarious, including diversification, professional management, convenience, and liquidity. Mutual funds provide diversification because they invest in various assets, which helps spread risk and reduce the impact of market volatility. Additionally, mutual funds are managed by seasoned fund managers with expertise in selecting and managing the fund's assets, which saves investors time and money. Mutual funds also offer convenience, as they enable investors to access a diverse range of assets with a single investment. Furthermore, mutual funds are highly liquid, making it easy for investors to buy and sell their shares as needed.

Essentially, like every investment, mutual funds carry some risks, such as market risk, management risk, and expense risk. Market risk implies that the fund's portfolio's value may rise or fall depending on market conditions. The performance of a mutual fund relies on the skill of the fund manager, which makes management risk a significant concern for investors. Finally, mutual funds charge fees to manage the fund, which can affect the overall performance of the fund, thus impacting the investor's return.

Types of mutual funds

Stock or equity funds: These funds invest in a diverse portfolio of stocks, with the goal of generating returns through capital appreciation and/or dividends.

> **Example**: The Fidelity Contrafund is a stock or equity fund that invests in a diverse portfolio of large and mid-sized companies with the goal of generating

returns through capital appreciation and dividends.

Bond or fixed income funds: These funds invest in a variety of debt securities, such as corporate bonds, government bonds, and municipal bonds. The goal of these funds is to generate income through regular interest payments.

> **Example**: The PIMCO Total Return Fund is a bond or fixed income fund that invests in a variety of debt securities, including corporate bonds, government bonds, and municipal bonds. The goal of this fund is to generate income through regular interest payments.

Balanced funds: These funds invest in a mix of stocks and bonds, with the goal of achieving a balance between income and growth.

> **Example**: The T. Rowe Price Balanced Fund is a balanced fund that invests in a mix of stocks and bonds with the goal of achieving a balance between income and growth.

Money market funds: These funds invest in short-term, high-quality debt securities, such as Treasury bills and commercial paper. They are designed to provide investors with a low-risk option for preserving capital and earning a modest return.

> **Example**: The Vanguard Prime Money Market Fund is a money market fund that invests in short-term, high-quality debt

securities such as Treasury bills and commercial paper.

Sector funds: These funds focus on a specific sector or industry, such as technology or healthcare. They can be more risky than diversified funds, as they are concentrated in a particular area and may be more vulnerable to economic or industry-specific risks.

> **Example**: The Technology Select Sector SPDR Fund is a sector fund that focuses on investing in technology companies.

International or global funds: These funds invest in stocks, bonds, or other securities from around the world. They offer investors the opportunity to diversify their portfolio and potentially benefit from economic growth in different countries.

> **Example**: Vanguard Total International Stock ETF is a global fund that invests in stocks, bonds, and other securities from around the world.

Index funds: These funds track the performance of a specific index, such as the S&P 500 or the NASDAQ Composite. They offer investors a low-cost way to gain exposure to a broad market or specific sector.

> **Example**: The Vanguard S&P 500 Index Fund is an index fund that tracks the performance of the S&P 500 Index.

Target-date funds: These funds are designed for investors with a specific retirement date in mind. The fund's asset allocation becomes more conservative as the target date approaches, shifting from stocks to bonds to provide income during retirement.

>**Example**: The Vanguard Target Retirement 2055 Fund is a target-date fund that is designed for investors with a retirement date of 2055.

Actively managed funds: These funds are managed by professional money managers who make decisions about which securities to buy and sell based on their own research and analysis. These funds may have higher fees than index funds, as they require more labor and expertise to manage.

>**Example**: The Fidelity Magellan Fund is an actively managed fund that is managed by professional money managers.

Passive or index-tracking funds: These funds aim to replicate the performance of a specific index, such as the S&P 500, by holding a portfolio of securities that closely match the index. These funds typically have lower fees than actively managed funds, as they do not require as much labor and expertise to manage.

>**Example**: The Vanguard S&P 500 ETF is a passive or index-tracking fund that aims to replicate the performance of the S&P 500 index.

Load funds: These mutual funds charge a fee, called a "load," to investors when they buy or sell shares of the fund. These fees can vary significantly, and may be assessed as a percentage of the investment amount or as a flat fee.

Example: Franklin Income Fund

No-load funds: These mutual funds do not charge a fee to investors when they buy or sell shares of the fund. These funds may have lower fees overall, as they do not need to charge a load to compensate for sales commissions.

Example: Vanguard Total Stock Market Index Fund

How to choose a mutual fund

- **Investment objective**: Determine your investment goals and risk tolerance, and look for mutual funds that align with your objectives. For example, if you are looking for income and stability, you may want to consider bond or fixed income funds, while if you are looking for growth, you may want to consider stock or equity funds.

- **Fund manager and track record**: Research the fund manager and their investment approach, as well as the fund's track record and historical performance. Look for managers with a proven track record of success and a consistent investment strategy.

- **Fees and expenses**: Carefully review the fees and expenses associated with the mutual fund, as these can impact your overall return on investment. Look for funds with low fees and expenses, as these can help to maximize your returns.

- **Diversification**: Consider diversifying your portfolio by investing in a mix of different types of mutual funds, such as stock, bond, and international funds. This can help to mitigate the impact of any one fund's performance on your overall investment portfolio.

- **Portfolio holdings**: Review the fund's portfolio holdings to understand the types of securities that the fund is investing in and how well diversified the portfolio is.

- **Investment style**: Consider the investment style of the fund, such as whether it is an actively managed fund or an index-tracking fund. Actively managed funds may offer the opportunity for outperformance, but they may also have higher fees and be more vulnerable to fund manager error. Index-tracking funds may offer lower fees and a more predictable investment strategy, but may not outperform the market.

- **Fund size and liquidity**: Consider the size and liquidity of the fund, as larger, more liquid funds may be more stable and easier to buy and sell.

- **Fund structure**: Different mutual funds may have different legal structures, such as open-ended or closed-end funds. Open-ended funds allow investors to buy and sell shares at any time, while closed-end funds have a fixed number of shares that are traded on an exchange.

- **Tax considerations**: Mutual funds may generate income or capital gains that are subject to taxation. Consider the tax implications of different funds and choose ones that align with your tax planning goals.

- **Investment minimums**: Some mutual funds may have minimum investment requirements, which may be a barrier for some investors. Consider whether the minimum investment is feasible for your financial situation.

- **Fund ratings and rankings**: Ratings agencies and financial publications may provide ratings and rankings for mutual funds. These can be a useful resource for comparing different funds, but it is important to remember that ratings and rankings are subjective and may not necessarily reflect the performance of a fund in the future.

- **Investment horizon**: Consider the length of time that you plan to hold your investment in the mutual fund. Some funds may be more suitable for long-term investments, while others may be more suitable for short-term trading.

Examples:

John wants to invest in a mutual fund that focuses on growth stocks. He chooses the XYZ Growth Fund, which invests in a diversified portfolio of large and mid-cap stocks that have the potential for long-term capital appreciation. The fund has a moderate risk level and charges an annual expense ratio of 1.5%.

Mary is looking for a mutual fund that provides a steady stream of income. She chooses the ABC Income Fund, which invests in a mix of corporate and government bonds with different maturities. The fund has a low risk level and charges an annual expense ratio of 0.8%.

Bill is looking for a mutual fund that provides a combination of growth and income. He chooses the DEF Balanced Fund, which invests in a mix of stocks and bonds with the goal of achieving both capital appreciation and income. The fund has a moderate risk level and charges an annual expense ratio of 1.2%.

Sarah is looking for a safe investment to park her cash while she decides how to allocate it. She chooses the GHI Money Market Fund, which invests in short-term, highly liquid debt securities such as Treasuries and commercial paper. The fund has a low risk level and charges an annual expense ratio of 0.5%.

In conclusion, each mutual fund has a unique investment objective, risk level, and fee structure, and understanding these factors is essential to identify the right investment opportunity. By examining these examples, investors can gain insight into the importance of evaluating and selecting the right mutual fund, leading to informed investment decisions.

Useful resources to analyze Mutual Funds

The Mutual Fund Observer: This independent site provides monthly commentary, news, and original research on mutual funds. It also maintains an active forum where investors can share insights and experiences.

Morningstar.com: A leading investment research company that offers detailed information about mutual funds, including performance history, risk rating, expense ratio, and portfolio holdings. Morningstar also provides a comprehensive mutual fund screener tool that lets investors search for funds based on specific criteria.

Bloomberg.com: Bloomberg provides extensive financial data and news, including mutual fund performance, market updates, and fund manager commentary. It also provides in-depth analysis and research on individual mutual funds.

Yahoo Finance: Yahoo's financial portal offers a wealth of data on mutual funds, including performance history, fund ratings, and top holdings. It also has a useful mutual fund screener for investors.

SEC EDGAR Database: The U.S. Securities and Exchange Commission's EDGAR database provides free access to mutual fund prospectuses and shareholder reports. This is an essential resource for investors looking to conduct a deep dive into a mutual fund's operations, fees, and investment strategy.

FundVisualizer: This tool allows investors to compare and analyze mutual funds. It includes features like side-by-side comparisons, portfolio overlap analysis, and performance scatter plots.

Avoiding Common Pitfalls

One of the most significant mistakes investors make is focusing solely on past performance. While past performance is an essential indicator of future success, it should not be the only consideration. Investment objectives, risk level, and fees are equally important factors that must be carefully evaluated before making a decision.

Fees are another essential consideration that many investors overlook. While they may seem small at first, the impact of fees on returns can be significant over time. It is vital to evaluate the fees associated with a mutual fund and to ensure that they align with investment goals and risk tolerance.

Risk is inherent in all investments, and mutual funds are no exception. Overlooking the risk associated with a mutual fund can lead to significant financial losses. Evaluating the risk level of a mutual fund is critical in determining the potential for long-term growth and success.

Investors often make the mistake of focusing on a single factor, such as a high dividend yield, while overlooking other important factors such as risk level and fees. Taking a comprehensive approach to evaluation, by considering all factors together, can lead to better-informed investment decisions.

Finally, regular review and adjustment of mutual fund investments is essential to long-term success. Market conditions change, and a mutual fund that was performing well in the past may not continue to do so. Regular review can help investors identify underperforming funds and make the necessary adjustments.

Summary

The mutual fund, a wondrous union of resources, brings together the aspirations of multiple investors to create a diversified portfolio of securities that can accomplish a specific objective.

While mutual funds offer a host of benefits, including professional management, liquidity, and diversification, avoiding common mistakes is essential. Investors must not solely depend on past performance but instead consider investment objectives, risk levels, and fees associated with the fund. By regularly reviewing and adapting investments to market conditions and taking a comprehensive approach to evaluation, investors can make informed investment decisions and aim for long-term success.

Chapter 11

Exchange Traded Funds (ETF'S) and Index Funds

In the vibrant sphere of investments, Exchange Traded Funds (ETFs) and Index Funds emerge as sophisticated instruments that cater to the discerning investor.

Exchange-traded funds (ETFs) elegant in their design, trace the intricate patterns of indices, commodities, or curated collections of assets, parading their allure on the grand stage of stock exchanges. They present a convenient and cost-effective portal for investors to delve into the rich tapestry of diverse assets, such as stocks, bonds, commodities, and currencies, without the necessity of procuring each asset individually.

> **Example**: The SPDR S&P 500 ETF, which tracks the performance of the S&P 500 index. This index is made up of 500 large-cap US companies, representing a broad cross-section of industries. By purchasing shares in the SPDR S&P 500 ETF, investors can gain exposure to the overall performance of the S&P 500 index without having to buy individual stocks in each of the 500 companies.

Index funds, though bearing a resemblance to ETFs in their pursuit of tracking an index's performance, reveal their distinct nature as mutual funds. These funds harbor a meticulously chosen assortment of assets, such as stocks or bonds, designed to reflect the composition of the underlying index with remarkable precision.

Example: The Vanguard 500 Index Fund, which tracks the performance of the S&P 500 index.

In the venerated dominion of investments, ETFs and index funds present a multitude of benefits that cater to a range of investor preferences. These advantages include diversification, professional management, cost-efficiency, and liquidity. By spreading risk across a broad range of securities, the diversification offered by these investment vehicles helps reduce the impact of market volatility. Additionally, expert management of these funds ensures that investors' portfolios are in the hands of experienced professionals who are skilled in selecting and managing securities.

Furthermore, ETFs and index funds generally have lower expense ratios compared to actively managed mutual funds, making them a cost-effective choice for investment. Lastly, the liquidity provided by these funds allows investors to easily buy and sell shares as needed, offering a level of flexibility.

Nevertheless, despite the many benefits of ETFs and index funds, they do come with risks. These funds are exposed to market risk, meaning the value of the fund's portfolio may fluctuate depending on market conditions. Moreover, the performance of an ETF or index fund may not exactly mirror the performance of the underlying index due to factors such as expenses and trading costs. As a result, investors should be aware of these risks and take a comprehensive approach to evaluating all factors when making investment decisions, in order to mitigate potential losses.

Key distinctions between ETFs and Index funds

In the universe of investments, ETFs and index funds both present their unique nuances, each appealing to the discerning investor in its own manner. Notable distinctions between these two investment vehicles arise from the manner in which they traverse the financial landscape.

- ETFs journey through the bustling marketplace, akin to stocks, enabling investors to acquire and relinquish their shares throughout the day. This flexibility allows investors to react to market fluctuations in real-time, a characteristic that distinguishes ETFs from their index fund counterparts.

- Index funds, on the other hand, adopt a more measured pace, setting their prices merely once per day as the market draws to a close. This singular daily pricing lends a sense of stability and consistency, in contrast to the dynamic nature of ETFs.

- When considering trading costs, ETFs may be subject to higher expenses due to the brokerage fees that accompany the purchase and sale of their shares.

- Index funds, however, often offer a more cost-efficient alternative, as they can be acquired and divested directly through the fund company, thus circumventing the need for brokerage fees.

In the grand tapestry of investments, both ETFs and index funds weave their own intricate patterns, and understanding their key distinctions can empower investors to make informed decisions that align with their unique financial goals.

Types of ETFs

Equity ETFs: These ETFs invest in stocks and aim to replicate the performance of a particular market index.

> **Example**: The Vanguard S&P 500 ETF tracks the performance of the S&P 500 index and offers investors broad exposure to the 500 largest US companies.

- BMO S&P/TSX Capped Composite Index ETF tracks the performance of the S&P/TSX Capped Composite Index, which includes a broad range of Canadian stocks.

- Vanguard FTSE All-World ex-Canada ETF tracks the performance of the FTSE All-World ex-Canada Index, which includes stocks and bonds from developed and emerging markets around the world, excluding Canada.

Bond ETFs: These ETFs invest in bonds and aim to replicate the performance of a particular bond index.

> **Example**: The iShares Core U.S. Aggregate Bond ETF tracks the performance of the Barclays Capital U.S. Aggregate Bond Index, which includes a broad range of investment-grade bonds.

Inverse ETFs: These ETFs aim to achieve the **opposite performance** of a particular index or benchmark. They can be used by investors as a **hedge** or to speculate on market movements.

> **Example**: The ProShares Short S&P 500 ETF aims to track the inverse performance of the S&P 500 index, meaning that **it aims to move in the opposite direction** of the S&P 500.

Commodity ETFs: These ETFs invest in physical commodities, such as gold or oil, or in futures contracts for commodities.

> **Example**: The SPDR Gold Shares ETF holds physical gold as an investment and aims to track the performance of the price of gold.

Currency ETFs: These ETFs invest in foreign currencies and aim to replicate the performance of a particular currency index.

> **Example**: The WisdomTree Bloomberg Dollar Bullish Fund tracks the performance of the Bloomberg Dollar Spot Index, which

measures the strength of the US dollar against a basket of major currencies.

Sector ETFs: These ETFs invest in a particular sector, such as technology or healthcare, and aim to replicate the performance of a particular sector index.

> **Example**: The Invesco QQQ Trust tracks the performance of the NASDAQ-100 index, which consists of 100 of the largest non-financial companies listed on the NASDAQ stock exchange.

Actively managed ETFs: Unlike index funds, which aim to replicate the performance of a particular index, actively managed ETFs are managed by a portfolio manager who makes decisions about which assets to include in the ETF.

> **Example**: The PIMCO Active Bond ETF, which is managed by the PIMCO investment team and seeks to outperform the Bloomberg Barclays U.S. Aggregate Bond Index.

Real estate ETFs: These ETFs invest in real estate investment trusts (REITs) and other real estate assets, such as commercial properties or mortgage-backed securities.

> **Example**: The Vanguard Real Estate ETF invests in a diverse range of REITs and real estate-related companies.

Leveraged ETFs: These ETFs use financial instruments, such as futures contracts or options, to amplify the performance of a particular index or benchmark. They are designed for investors who want to take on more risk in an effort to achieve higher returns.

> **Example**: The ProShares Ultra S&P 500 ETF uses leverage to aim for twice the daily performance of the S&P 500 index.

Types of Index Funds

Equity index funds: These index funds invest in stocks and aim to replicate the performance of a particular market index.

> **Example**: The Vanguard 500 Index Fund tracks the performance of the S&P 500 index and offers investors broad exposure to the 500 largest US companies.

> - Vanguard FTSE Canada All Cap Index Fund encompasses a broad range of Canadian stocks.

Bond index funds: These index funds invest in bonds and aim to replicate the performance of a particular bond index.

> **Example**: The iShares Core U.S. Aggregate Bond ETF tracks the performance of the Barclays Capital U.S. Aggregate Bond Index, which includes a broad range of investment-grade bonds.

Balanced index funds: These index funds invest in a mix of stocks and bonds, aiming to provide a balance of growth and income.

> **Example**: The Vanguard Balanced Index Fund holds a mix of stocks and bonds and aims to track the performance of the CRSP US Balanced Index, which is a market-cap-weighted index of stocks and bonds.

Target-date index funds: These index funds invest in a mix of stocks, bonds, and other assets, and are designed for investors who have a specific retirement date in mind. The asset allocation of these funds is automatically adjusted as the target date approaches, becoming more conservative over time.

> **Example**: The Vanguard Target Retirement Fund is a series of target-date index funds that are designed for investors with a retirement date in a specific year. The asset allocation of these funds is automatically adjusted to become more conservative as the target date approaches.

International index funds: These index funds invest in stocks and bonds from countries outside the United States.

> **Example**: The Vanguard FTSE All-World ex-US Index Fund tracks the performance of the FTSE All-World ex-US Index, which includes stocks and bonds from developed and emerging markets around the world, excluding the United States.

Small-cap index funds: These index funds invest in small-cap stocks, which are stocks of companies with a small market capitalization. Small-cap stocks are generally considered to be riskier but also have the potential for higher returns.

> **Example**: The Vanguard Small-Cap Index Fund tracks the performance of the CRSP US Small Cap Index, which includes small-cap stocks from a broad range of industries.

Emerging markets index funds: These index funds invest in stocks and bonds from emerging markets, which are countries that are in the process of developing their economies. Emerging markets are generally considered to be riskier but also have the potential for higher returns.

> **Example**: The Vanguard Emerging Markets Stock Index Fund tracks the performance of the FTSE Emerging Markets Index, which includes stocks from emerging markets around the world.

How to choose ETFs and index funds

To gracefully navigate the territory of ETFs and index funds, the discerning investor must embark on a journey illuminated by a constellation of guiding principles:

- **Ascertain your investment objectives**: Prior to delving into the specifics of ETFs and index funds, clarify your aspirations for your investments. Ponder elements such as risk tolerance, time horizon, and your overall financial landscape.

- **Contemplate the fees**: While ETFs and index funds typically boast lower fees compared to actively managed mutual funds, it remains crucial to compare the costs of various options. Seek funds with modest expense ratios, as they will consume a smaller portion of your returns over time.

- **Examine the underlying assets**: Grasp the assets in which an ETF or index fund invests. Reflect upon aspects such as asset type (e.g., stocks, bonds), geographical location, and sector or industry.

- **Investigate the index or benchmark**: ETFs and index funds trace the path of a specific index or benchmark. Ensure that you comprehend the criteria employed in selecting the assets within the index and determine if they align with your investment aspirations.

- **Assess the track record**: Scrutinize the fund's historical performance to glean insights into its behavior amid diverse market conditions. Bear in mind that past performance may not foretell future outcomes.

- **Diversify your portfolio**: Strive for a balanced portfolio by allocating investments across a spectrum of assets. Utilize ETFs and index funds to achieve diversification, rather than solely investing in individual stocks.

- **Consult professional guidance**: For those new to investing or uncertain about which ETFs or index funds to select, enlisting the expertise of a financial advisor or professional can be invaluable. They can assist you in making well-informed decisions tailored to your unique investment goals and risk tolerance.

Examples:

Example 1: Lisa is interested in investing in the technology sector. She chooses the ABC Technology ETF, which tracks the performance of a basket of tech stocks. The ETF charges an annual expense ratio of 0.5% and is currently trading at $100 per share. Lisa buys 50 shares for a total investment of $5,000.

Example 2: Bob is looking for a bond ETF with a high credit rating. He chooses the XYZ Corporate Bond ETF, which tracks the performance of a basket of investment-grade corporate bonds. The ETF charges an annual expense ratio of 0.3% and is currently trading at $50 per share. Bob buys 100 shares for a total investment of $5,000.

Example 3: Jane is looking for an index fund that provides diversification across different asset classes. She chooses the DEF Balanced Index Fund, which tracks the performance of a diversified portfolio of stocks and bonds. The index fund charges an annual expense ratio of 0.8% and is currently trading at $25 per share. Jane buys 100 shares for a total investment of $2,500.

Example 4: Mary is looking for a low-cost way to invest in the S&P 500. She chooses the GHI S&P 500 Index Fund, which tracks the performance of the S&P 500 index. The index fund charges an annual expense ratio of 0.1% and is currently trading at $100 per share. Mary buys 50 shares for a total investment of $5,000.

In the stipulated examples, Lisa opts for a technology-focused stock ETF, Bob selects an investment-grade corporate bond ETF, Jane invests in a balanced index fund that diversifies across asset classes, and Mary chooses a stock index fund tracking the S&P 500. Each investment follows the performance of a distinct index or asset class, offering diversification, professional management, and cost efficiency. Nonetheless, they remain subject to market risk and tracking error, which investors must weigh when determining the most suitable investment strategy for their financial goals and risk profile.

Useful resources to analyze ETFs and Index Funds

ETF Database: ETF Database is an investment research firm dedicated to helping investors understand and utilize ETFs. Their database includes ETF fundamentals, performance, and analysis, along with tools for screening and comparison.

ETF.com: ETF.com is a leading authority on news, data, and analysis about the universe of ETFs. The website provides in-depth research, ratings, and performance metrics on individual ETFs, and its ETF screener tool allows investors to search based on various criteria.

Morningstar.com: Morningstar offers extensive data and research tools for ETFs and index funds, including fund ratings, yields, performance, and underlying holdings. Their premium service provides advanced analysis capabilities.

Yahoo Finance: The site includes a dedicated ETF section that includes market data, a screener, and a comparison tool. It also provides comprehensive financial data, news, and analysis for thousands of ETFs and index funds.

Seeking Alpha: Seeking Alpha is a crowd-sourced content service for financial markets. Articles and blogs by financial analysts and investors cover a broad spectrum of ETFs and index funds, offering insights that can be helpful for both fundamental and technical analysis.

Investopedia: While not offering specific analysis, Investopedia is a trusted resource for learning about ETFs and index funds, their strategies, and how they differ. It also offers tutorials, guides, and explanatory articles to help investors make more informed decisions.

Avoiding Common Pitfalls

Neglecting Investment Goals and Risk Tolerance: One of the most frequent errors investors make is failing to align their ETF and index fund selections with their investment goals and risk tolerance. Before embarking on this journey, ensure that you have a clear understanding of your objectives, time horizon, and risk appetite, and choose funds that align with these considerations.

Overlooking Expense Ratios and Trading Costs: In the pursuit of investment success, many overlook the impact of expense ratios and trading costs on their returns. While ETFs and index funds typically boast lower fees than their actively managed counterparts, it is crucial to compare these costs across available options. Select funds with modest expense ratios and trading costs to optimize your returns over time.

Insufficient Diversification: A well-balanced investment portfolio should encompass a diverse array of assets, sectors, and geographical regions. Investors sometimes fall into the trap of focusing too narrowly on specific sectors or themes, resulting in inadequate diversification. Avoid this pitfall by choosing a mix of ETFs and index funds that provide broad exposure across various asset classes and regions.

Misinterpreting Fund Objectives and Holdings: Misunderstanding the objectives and holdings of a particular ETF or index fund can lead to unintended consequences. It is essential to thoroughly examine the fund's prospectus and asset allocation to ensure that it aligns with your investment strategy and desired risk profile.

Succumbing to Market Noise and Emotional Investing: The investment journey is often fraught with market noise and emotional reactions, which can lead to hasty and ill-informed decisions. Resist the temptation to react impulsively to market fluctuations or chase after recent top-performing funds, as this approach rarely leads to long-term success. Instead, maintain a disciplined and well-reasoned strategy, guided by your investment goals and risk tolerance.

Failing to Monitor and Rebalance: The passage of time and the ebb and flow of market dynamics may cause your portfolio's initial allocation to drift. Neglecting to monitor and rebalance your investments can result in a misalignment with your desired risk profile and long-term objectives. Regularly review your ETF and index fund holdings, making adjustments as needed to maintain a well-balanced and diversified portfolio.

Summary

In the vast landscape of investment opportunities, Exchange Traded Funds and Index Funds weave together a tapestry of potential and diversification. Their intricate architecture provides a harmonious fusion of convenience and cost-effectiveness, all while granting access to a diverse array of assets such as stocks, bonds, commodities, and currencies.

It is of paramount importance to acknowledge the delicate equilibrium that resides within these investment vehicles. The interplay between ETFs and Index Funds, which share commonalities yet possess their own distinct qualities, calls for our careful attention and discernment. In selecting the perfect instrument to achieve our financial ambitions, we must traverse the terrain of risk and return, fortified by knowledge and guided by experience.

Chapter 12

Foreign Exchange (Forex)

The foreign exchange market, commonly referred to as Forex or FX, is the global arena in which currencies are exchanged and traded. This dynamic process of currency conversion serves as a vital mechanism for facilitating international trade and investment.

Forex investing involves the strategic buying and selling of currencies with the objective of capitalizing on fluctuations in exchange rates. As the world's largest and most liquid financial market, trillions of dollars are transacted daily, making it an attractive option for investors.

There are several advantages to investing in the Forex market. Its high liquidity ensures that currencies can be easily bought and sold with minimal impact on market prices. Additionally, the market's flexibility allows for round-the-clock trading, offering investors the freedom to engage at their convenience. Forex brokers often provide leverage, enabling investors to trade with greater capital than they possess, potentially increasing returns while also amplifying risks. Lastly, foreign exchange investments can contribute to portfolio diversification, mitigating the overall risk associated with investments.

However, investors should also be mindful of the various risks inherent to the Forex market.

Currency values are subject to fluctuations due to economic and political events, which can directly impact the worth of an investment. Political risks, such as changes in government policies or instability within a country, may also influence a currency's value. Furthermore, economic indicators like gross domestic product (GDP) and unemployment rates can affect currency values. The Forex market is known for its volatility, which can result in significant price swings and increased risk for investors.

It is also imperative to exercise caution, as fraudulent individuals and companies may attempt to exploit investors within the Forex market. Conducting thorough research and partnering only with reputable brokers and financial advisors is essential for safeguarding one's interests in this complex financial landscape.

An Overview of Currency Pairs in the Forex Market

In the vast landscape of global finance, the foreign exchange (Forex) market holds a prominent position, showcasing an array of currency pairs. These pairs represent the core of international trade and investment, reflecting the dynamic relationships between global economies. From the most frequently traded to the lesser-known, each currency pair exhibits distinct characteristics, contributing to the diverse composition of the world's largest and most liquid financial market.

The Majors: Dominant Players:

At the forefront of the Forex market, the Major currency pairs are the most traded and influential. Comprising the world's leading currencies, including the US Dollar (USD), Euro (EUR), Japanese Yen (JPY), British Pound (GBP), Swiss Franc (CHF), Canadian Dollar (CAD), and Australian Dollar (AUD), the Majors represent the pulse of global economic power. Their relationships form pairs such as EUR/USD, USD/JPY, GBP/USD, and USD/CHF, each reflecting the intricate interplay between their respective economies. These pairs are popular among traders and investors due to their vast liquidity, tight spreads, and the abundance of information available, enabling them to navigate the ever-changing global financial landscape.

The Crosses: A Diverse Array:

While the Majors dominate the Forex market, the Crosses introduce a wider variety of currency pairings that do not involve the US Dollar. These pairs, such as EUR/JPY, GBP/JPY, or AUD/CAD, offer investors a broader view of the global economy and provide opportunities to explore unique trading strategies and gain exposure to different regions. The Crosses exhibit a complex interrelationship, each with its own story, revealing the subtle intricacies of international economic connections and regional developments.

The Exotics: Exploring Uncharted Territory:

In the farthest reaches of the Forex market, the Exotic currency pairs involve currencies from emerging markets or smaller economies, such as the Mexican Peso (MXN), South African Rand (ZAR), or Thai Baht (THB). These pairs are less familiar, have more unpredictable movements, and often possess limited liquidity. However, it is within these Exotic pairs that traders may uncover potentially rewarding opportunities, providing the chance for higher returns and portfolio diversification. The Exotics also come with increased risk, as their volatility and vulnerability to external factors can lead to sudden, significant fluctuations in their performance.

The Forex market's currency pairs form a diverse array of opportunities, highlighting the interconnected nature of the global economy. As traders and investors explore this intricate landscape, they may uncover a wealth of possibilities, each currency pair offering unique opportunities that reflect the constant evolution of international trade and investment.

How to choose Foreign Exchange (Forex) investments

- **Comprehend the risks**: Forex investing involves unique risks such as currency risk, political risk, and economic risk. Ensure a profound understanding of these risks and their potential impact on your investments. For instance, monitor geopolitical news to understand how political events might influence currency value.

- **Opt for a reputable broker**: A reliable broker is crucial in Forex investing. Seek a broker regulated by a reputable organization, such as the Financial Conduct Authority (FCA) or the Commodity Futures Trading Commission (CFTC), and with an established industry reputation.

- **Assess the fees**: Brokers' fees vary and can influence your returns. Understand the fee structure associated with your preferred broker to make an informed decision. Compare brokers like IG, Forex.com, and Saxo Bank to determine which one best suits your needs.

- **Evaluate the trading platform**: The trading platform significantly affects your investment experience. Opt for one that is user-friendly and possesses the necessary features for making informed decisions. Platforms like MetaTrader 4, MetaTrader 5, and cTrader are popular choices.

- **Utilize a demo account**: Many brokers provide demo accounts, enabling you to practice trading using virtual funds before investing real money. This can help familiarize you with the Forex market and test various investment strategies.

- **Implement risk management strategies**: Employ strategies to manage risk in Forex investing, such as setting stop-loss orders, diversifying your portfolio, and using leverage judiciously.

- **Remain informed**: Stay updated on economic and political events that may impact your investments. Monitor reputable news sources and market analysis, and consider consulting with a financial advisor or professional trader. Resources like Forex Factory and DailyFX provide valuable insights.

- **Ascertain your risk tolerance**: Determine your level of comfort with the inherent risks of Forex investing. Take into account your financial situation, investment objectives, and personal risk tolerance when deciding on the extent of your foreign exchange investments.

- **Apply technical and fundamental analysis**: Technical analysis relies on historical price and volume data to predict future price movements, while fundamental analysis examines economic and political factors that may affect a currency's value. Both methods can aid in making informed investment decisions in the Forex market.

- **Select appropriate currency pairs**: With hundreds of currency pairs available for trading, choose pairs that align with your investment goals and risk tolerance. For example, if seeking long-term growth, consider pairs with higher potential returns but also increased volatility, such as GBP/JPY or AUD/NZD.

- **Regularly review your portfolio**: Assess your Forex portfolio regularly to ensure it aligns with your investment objectives and risk tolerance. Make necessary adjustments to maintain a balanced and diversified portfolio. Tools like Myfxbook can help with portfolio tracking and analysis.

Examples:

Example 1: Diversification and Hedging

John, an experienced stock market investor, is looking to diversify his investment portfolio to protect against potential losses in the stock market. He decides to invest in the Forex market to take advantage of its unique characteristics, such as high liquidity and round-the-clock trading. By investing in currency pairs that have a low correlation with his stock investments, John can hedge his portfolio against economic events that could negatively impact his stock positions.

For instance, John holds stocks in American technology companies that may be negatively affected by a weak US economy. To hedge this risk, he decides to invest in the EUR/USD currency pair, expecting that the Euro will appreciate against the US Dollar if the US economy weakens.

Example 2: Capitalizing on Interest Rate Differentials

Susan, an experienced Forex trader, is looking to capitalize on interest rate differentials between countries. She notices that the Reserve Bank of Australia (RBA) has a higher interest rate than the Bank of Japan (BOJ). Based on this information, she decides to go long on the AUD/JPY currency pair, which means she buys Australian Dollars and sells Japanese Yen.

The interest rate differential between the two countries allows Susan to earn a positive carry trade. As long as the AUD remains stable or appreciates against the JPY, she will earn interest on her long position. Susan monitors economic indicators and central bank announcements to ensure her position remains profitable.

Example 3: Taking Advantage of Market Volatility

Tom, a day trader, seeks to profit from short-term market fluctuations in the Forex market. He closely follows economic and political news that might influence currency values, and uses technical analysis to identify potential trading opportunities.

One day, Tom sees that the European Central Bank (ECB) is about to announce its monetary policy decision. He anticipates that the announcement might cause volatility in the EUR/USD currency pair. Based on his technical analysis, Tom identifies key support and resistance levels for the EUR/USD pair.

He prepares a trading strategy with stop-loss orders and take-profit targets, depending on various potential outcomes of the announcement.

As the announcement is released, the ECB unexpectedly decides to cut interest rates. This decision leads to a sharp drop in the value of the Euro against the US Dollar. Tom had previously placed a short position on the EUR/USD currency pair at a resistance level of 1.2000, with a stop-loss order at 1.2050 and a take-profit target at 1.1900. As the market reacts to the news, the EUR/USD pair falls to his take-profit target, allowing Tom to capitalize on the short-term price movement resulting from the ECB announcement.

Example 4: Profiting from Currency Strength and Weakness

Anna, a swing trader, analyzes the strength and weakness of various currencies to identify potential trading opportunities in the Forex market. She frequently studies economic indicators, such as GDP growth, inflation, and employment data, as well as central bank policies.

Anna notices that the US economy is showing signs of strength, with robust GDP growth, low unemployment, and the Federal Reserve signaling potential interest rate hikes. On the other hand, she observes that the Canadian economy is facing headwinds due to falling oil prices and sluggish GDP growth. Based on this fundamental analysis, Anna believes that the US Dollar will appreciate against the Canadian Dollar.

She decides to go long on the USD/CAD currency pair, buying US Dollars and selling Canadian Dollars. She enters the trade at 1.3000 and sets a stop-loss order at 1.2900 to protect her position. Anna places a take-profit target at 1.3200, expecting that the strength of the US economy and the weakness of the Canadian economy will push the USD/CAD pair higher.

Over the next few weeks, the USD/CAD pair appreciates, and Anna's take-profit target is reached, allowing her to profit from the currency strength and weakness she identified through her fundamental analysis.

Useful resources to analyze Foreign Exchange

Forex.com: Forex.com is one of the largest forex brokers, providing traders with a robust platform for trading in the foreign exchange markets. They also offer a variety of research tools, charts, news, and analysis that can help traders in decision-making.

DailyFX: DailyFX is a website run by the forex broker IG, which provides comprehensive coverage of the forex market. It offers news updates, market analysis, charts, educational resources, and forex trading signals. Their analysis covers both technical and fundamental aspects of forex trading.

Bank for International Settlements (BIS): The BIS is an international financial organization serving as a bank for central banks. They publish a wealth of information related to the forex markets, including triennial surveys detailing global forex market activity.

Investing.com: Investing.com offers a wide range of financial data and tools, including real-time and historical forex rates for a multitude of currency pairs. It also provides analysis, news, an economic calendar, and other resources that are useful for forex traders.

XE.com: XE is widely known for its comprehensive currency converter tool, but it also provides forex news, currency charts, and rate alerts. It's a useful resource for getting a quick overview of market conditions and tracking exchange rates.

MetaTrader: MetaTrader is a trading platform used by many forex traders. While it's not a resource in the traditional sense, it offers a wide variety of tools for analyzing the forex market, including technical indicators, charting tools, and the ability to backtest trading strategies.

Avoiding Common Pitfalls

In the intricate realm of the foreign exchange (Forex) market, every investor must tread carefully to avoid the pitfalls that may hinder their journey towards financial success. These obstacles often emerge from misconceptions, misguided strategies, and a lack of understanding.

Insufficient Market Knowledge: A firm grasp of the fundamentals and inner workings of the Forex market is crucial for any investor. A lack of understanding can lead to ill-informed decisions and potential losses. To avoid this pitfall, educate yourself on the various aspects of Forex trading, including currency pairs, market mechanics, and economic factors that influence currency values.

Inadequate Risk Management: Risk is an inherent part of Forex investing, and a failure to manage it effectively can result in significant financial loss. To mitigate risk, implement strategies such as setting stop-loss orders, diversifying your portfolio, and using leverage judiciously. Be mindful of your risk tolerance and adjust your trading approach accordingly.

Overtrading: The allure of the Forex market can tempt investors to trade excessively, leading to a lack of focus and increased exposure to risk. To prevent overtrading, establish a well-defined trading plan with clear objectives, and adhere to it diligently. Regularly assess your trading performance to ensure it aligns with your goals and risk tolerance.

Emotional Decision-Making: Emotions can cloud your judgment and lead to impulsive decisions that undermine your trading strategy. Cultivate emotional discipline by developing a systematic approach to trading, maintaining a clear mindset, and avoiding emotional triggers such as fear, greed, or overconfidence.

Reliance on Unreliable Trading Systems: In the pursuit of profitable investments, some investors may fall prey to unproven or untrustworthy trading systems. This can lead to a false sense of security and ultimately, financial loss. Thoroughly research and test any trading system before committing to it, and only rely on reputable sources of information and advice.

Neglecting Ongoing Education: The Forex market is constantly evolving, and a successful investor must adapt and grow alongside it. Neglecting ongoing education can result in outdated knowledge and ineffective trading strategies. Stay informed by following reputable news sources, participating in educational webinars, and engaging in Forex forums or communities.

Unrealistic Expectations: Forex investing, like any other form of investment, does not guarantee instant success or immediate wealth. Setting unrealistic expectations can lead to frustration and impulsive decision-making. Approach Forex investing with patience and a long-term perspective, recognizing that success requires dedication, discipline, and continuous learning.

Summary

In the dominion of Forex investing, navigating the challenges and opportunities inherent in this global financial market demands essential insights. Understanding the diverse array of currency pairs and adopting suitable investment strategies are crucial for investors. Emphasizing market knowledge, risk management, and emotional discipline, the pursuit of financial success becomes attainable.

Moreover, recognizing the importance of avoiding common pitfalls that may obstruct progress in the Forex market is vital. By highlighting the need for continuous education, realistic expectations, and adherence to a well-defined trading plan, investors can better equip themselves to make informed decisions and seize the opportunities that the ever-evolving Forex market presents.

Chapter 13

Cryptocurrencies and Non-fungible tokens (NFTs)

In the universe of digital marvels, cryptocurrencies and non-fungible tokens (NFTs) interweave to paint a vivid arras of innovation and potential. These ethereal currencies, unshackled from the confines of traditional institutions, dance to the rhythm of decentralization. Their essence, encrypted within the vast expanse of the blockchain, illuminates a path toward a transparent and secure future.

Cryptocurrencies pirouette in the digital world, enabling seamless transactions unfettered by the chains of bureaucracy. Unbound by the corporeal realm, they exist as intangible whispers, their value determined by the collective belief in their worth.

NFTs, on the other hand, embody the essence of uniqueness, each representing a singular digital treasure—an artwork, a collectible, a singular moment in time.

United, these digital marvels journey through the virtual wilderness, their tracks permanently etched onto the unyielding stone of the blockchain. In this boundless digital landscape, transactions dart with the swiftness and grace of an agile fox, undeterred by the cumbersome intervention of intermediaries.

As mesmerizing as their symphony may be, the universe of cryptocurrencies and NFTs carries its own set of somber notes. Their unpredictability is much like the crescendo of a powerful orchestra, soaring to euphoric highs before plunging into dramatic lows, leaving listeners in a constant state of suspense. The lack of oversight is like a composition without a conductor, an unguided harmony where each player determines their part. And hidden in the silence between the movements, cybersecurity risks lie in wait, prepared to disrupt the rhythm and fracture the delicate veil of tranquility.

In this sprawling landscape of digital innovation, cryptocurrencies and NFTs intersect, their appeal both captivating and powerful. However, as with any venture, one must carefully navigate the risks and uncertainties, while never losing sight of the inherent potential and benefits.

Types of Cryptocurrencies

Bitcoin: The pioneering and widely-recognized cryptocurrency, established in 2009, employs a decentralized, peer-to-peer network for seamless transactions, enabling online purchases and transfers without reliance on banks or financial institutions.

Altcoins: Alternative cryptocurrencies to Bitcoin, often embodying similar traits but diverging in technical implementation or use cases. Notable examples include Ethereum, a decentralized platform for smart contracts; Litecoin, designed for enhanced speed and efficiency; and Monero, a privacy-centric cryptocurrency.

Stablecoins: Cryptocurrencies anchored to stable assets, such as the US dollar, aiming to provide price stability and mitigate volatility. Tether, pegged to the US dollar, and USD Coin, issued by a consortium of financial institutions, exemplify stablecoins.

Security tokens: Cryptocurrencies representing asset ownership, like real estate or company stocks, often regulated as investment forms. For instance, purchasing a security token tied to commercial real estate ownership could yield a share of the property's profits.

Utility tokens: Cryptocurrencies granting access to specific products or services, frequently used for payment within designated platforms or ecosystems. Utility tokens may enable premium features on social media platforms or streaming service subscriptions.

Privacy coins: Cryptocurrencies emphasizing user anonymity and privacy, employing encryption and masking techniques. Zcash, utilizing zero-knowledge proofs, allows for concealed transactions and identities.

Central Bank Digital Currencies (CBDCs): Digital currencies issued by central banks, functioning similar to traditional fiat currencies but enabling peer-to-peer transactions.

Hybrid coins: Cryptocurrencies merging features from multiple types, such as a stablecoin with privacy and anonymity.

Masternode coins: Cryptocurrencies utilizing a masternode system for transactions and additional network functionality. Masternodes, specialized nodes performing specific tasks, often earn rewards for their network contributions.

Tokenized assets: Cryptocurrencies representing physical asset ownership, like gold or silver, facilitating digital purchase and trading without necessitating physical handling.

Decentralized Finance (DeFi): Cryptocurrencies employed within DeFi applications, blockchain-based financial services. DeFi coins may serve as payment or collateral, offering features like yield farming or governance rights.

Airdrop coins: Cryptocurrencies distributed freely to numerous users, often promoting adoption or projects. Airdrops typically involve marketing campaigns and may require user actions to receive coins.

Ethical coins: Cryptocurrencies supporting ethical or socially responsible causes, potentially funding environmental sustainability or social justice projects.

Social media coins: Cryptocurrencies integrated with social media platforms, serving as payment methods or rewarding content creation and sharing.

Gaming coins: Cryptocurrencies used in the gaming industry for payments or in-game currency, purchasing virtual goods or services or participating in gaming tournaments.

Rewards coins: Cryptocurrencies used to incentivize user actions like surveys or tasks, driving behavior or collecting data.

Staking coins: Cryptocurrencies employing a Proof-of-Stake (PoS) consensus mechanism, necessitating users to hold specific amounts to participate in network validation. Users staking coins earn a portion of network-generated rewards.

Types of NFTs

Art NFTs: Digital art pieces, including digital paintings, drawings, sculptures, and various visual art forms, represented as NFTs and traded on multiple marketplaces.

Collectibles NFTs: Digital items designed for collection, such as virtual trading cards or sports memorabilia, often with limited edition runs and potentially high valuations.

Game items NFTs: Unique in-game items offered as NFTs, particularly in blockchain-based games, encompassing weapons, armor, and other advantageous items.

Virtual real estate NFTs: NFTs representing virtual real estate, like virtual land or properties within virtual worlds, tradable and potentially appreciating in value over time.

Music NFTs: NFTs featuring music, including streaming or downloading rights, exclusive merchandise, or experiences.

Identity NFTs: NFTs representing an individual's online identity or reputation, facilitating authenticity verification and tradable like other NFTs.

Utility NFTs: NFTs providing access to specific services or functions, such as club memberships or event access, monetizing exclusive experiences or services.

Domain NFTs: NFTs denoting ownership of specific domain names on the decentralized web ("Web3"), offering added security and ownership benefits.

Social media NFTs: NFTs employed by platforms like Twitter to monetize and reward popular content creators, representing ownership of tweets or posts and tradeable on the open market.

Meme NFTs: NFTs based on popular or original memes, allowing for unique meme versions or creations to be bought and sold.

Wearable NFTs: NFTs representing physical items like clothing or accessories, embedded with distinctive digital tokens, usable for verifying authenticity and provenance, and tradeable like other NFTs.

Experiential NFTs: NFTs symbolizing unique experiences or events, such as concert tickets or VIP access, monetizing and rewarding participation or contributions to specific experiences.

How to choose Cryptocurrencies and NFTs

- **Grasp the purpose of the cryptocurrency or NFT**: Understand the use case and functionality of the cryptocurrency or NFT in question. Evaluate whether it addresses a particular issue or garners a sizable, active user base. For instance, Bitcoin offers a decentralized digital currency, while Bored Ape Yacht Club NFTs have become a sought-after collectible series.

- **Investigate the team behind the project**: Examine the group responsible for the development and maintenance of the cryptocurrency or NFT. Assess their past successes, future plans, and responsiveness to the community. Resources like CoinGecko or CoinMarketCap can provide information on project teams.

- **Analyze the technology**: Examine the technology that underpins the cryptocurrency or NFT, including the blockchain platform and security measures. Ensure that the technology is reliable and secure. Platforms such as Ethereum and Solana are well-regarded for their technological foundations.

- **Assess liquidity and market demand**: Evaluate the liquidity and open market demand for the cryptocurrency or NFT. Determine the ease of buying and selling the asset. Platforms like Uniswap for cryptocurrencies and OpenSea for NFTs can provide insights into trading volumes and liquidity.

- **Comprehend the risks**: Recognize the volatility and risks associated with cryptocurrencies and NFTs, and prepare for potential price fluctuations.

- **Diversification**: Spread your investments across various cryptocurrencies and NFTs to mitigate risks.

- **Conduct independent research**: Avoid relying solely on others' advice when investing in cryptocurrencies and NFTs. Perform your own due diligence to comprehend the risks and potential rewards of an investment.

- **Familiarize yourself with fees**: Understand the fees associated with different cryptocurrencies and NFTs, such as transaction fees and mining fees, and how they may affect your investment returns.

- **Consider the regulatory landscape**: Understand the legal and regulatory implications of investing in cryptocurrencies and NFTs in your jurisdiction, as regulations may vary across countries.

- **Examine security measures**: Research the security measures in place to safeguard your investment, as cryptocurrencies and NFTs can be vulnerable to hacking and other cyber threats.

- **Explore storage and custody options**: Research the storage and custody options for cryptocurrencies and NFTs, such as online wallets like MetaMask or offline solutions like Ledger, and select the most suitable one for your needs.

- **Monitor market trends**: Keep track of market trends and sentiment for the cryptocurrency or NFT under consideration, comparing its performance and popularity to other assets in its category.

Examples:

Example 1: Cryptocurrency – Long-term Holding (HODLing)

Alice believes in the future potential of cryptocurrencies, specifically Bitcoin (BTC), as an alternative to traditional financial systems. She decides to invest a portion of her savings in Bitcoin as a long-term investment, known as HODLing (Hold on for Dear Life).

Alice purchases 1 Bitcoin at $20,000 and securely stores it in her hardware wallet. Over the years, the value of Bitcoin rises, and it reaches $100,000. By HODLing her Bitcoin, Alice has made a profit of $80,000 on her long-term investment in the cryptocurrency.

Example 2: Cryptocurrency – Trading Altcoins

Bob, an experienced trader, seeks to profit from the volatility of the cryptocurrency market by actively trading altcoins (alternative cryptocurrencies to Bitcoin). He researches various altcoins, analyzing their fundamentals, and uses technical analysis to identify potential entry and exit points for trades.

Bob spots an opportunity in the Ethereum (ETH) market, as it is set to release a significant update to its network. He believes that this update will increase demand for the cryptocurrency. Bob buys 10 ETH at $2,000 each and sets a stop-loss order at $1,800 to protect his investment. He sets a take-profit target at $2,500, expecting that the update will have a positive impact on the price of Ethereum.

After the successful network update, the price of ETH rises to $2,500, and Bob's take-profit order is executed, netting him a profit of $5,000 on his altcoin trade.

Example 3: NFT – Digital Art Collection

Carla has a keen interest in digital art and wants to invest in non-fungible tokens (NFTs) representing unique pieces of digital artwork. She researches various NFT marketplaces and artists, ultimately deciding to purchase an NFT of a limited-edition digital painting by a well-known artist.

Carla spends 1 ETH (valued at $2,000) to buy the digital art NFT. Over time, the artist's popularity grows, and the demand for their limited edition NFTs increases. Carla receives an offer of 5 ETH (valued at $10,000) for her digital art NFT and decides to sell it, making a profit of 4 ETH (equivalent to $8,000) on her NFT investment.

Example 4: NFT – Virtual Real Estate

David has been following the development of various metaverse platforms where users can buy, sell, and develop virtual land. He decides to invest in virtual real estate, purchasing a plot of land in a popular metaverse platform.

David buys the virtual land NFT for 10 ETH (valued at $20,000). As the metaverse platform gains traction and attracts more users, the demand for virtual land increases. Eventually, David receives an offer of 20 ETH (valued at $40,000) for his virtual land NFT. He decides to sell it, making a profit of 10 ETH (equivalent to $20,000) on his virtual real estate investment.

Useful resources to analyze Cryptocurrencies and NFTs

CoinMarketCap.com: CoinMarketCap is a leading cryptocurrency website that provides a vast range of data about the crypto market. It offers real-time price tracking, market capitalization, trading volume, and historical data for all major cryptocurrencies. It also has a portfolio tracking app and resources for crypto education.

Messari.io: Messari offers reliable and comprehensive data, news, and research about the crypto market. Its tools include advanced screening capabilities that allow users to search for cryptocurrencies based on specific criteria. It also has a wide range of educational content about the blockchain and cryptocurrency industry.

CoinGecko.com: It is a cryptocurrency data platform that provides real-time and historical data on 6000+ digital currencies. It offers a comprehensive view of the market along with detailed coin analysis, price tracking, portfolio management, and a robust API for further data exploration.

NonFungible.com: A data analytics and market intelligence platform specifically focused on the non-fungible tokens (NFTs) sector. It provides insights into NFT market trends, sales history, volume, and rankings. It's an essential resource for those interested in understanding and navigating the world of NFTs.

OpenSea.io: A leading marketplace for NFTs where users can buy, sell, and explore digital assets like crypto art, virtual real estate, collectibles, and more. It provides historical sales data, rankings, and other insights about the NFT market.

CryptoCompare.com: It provides a comprehensive array of real-time and historical cryptocurrency market data. It offers charting tools, portfolio management, discussion forums, and a robust API for those looking to dive deep into cryptocurrency analysis.

Etherscan.io: Etherscan is an Ethereum blockchain explorer that provides detailed information about Ethereum-based tokens, transactions, and addresses. It is widely used for verifying transactions and researching activity on the Ethereum network, including that of NFTs and other Ethereum-based cryptocurrencies.

Blockchain.com: Blockchain.com is a versatile resource offering a crypto wallet, explorer, and a comprehensive data section with charts on various metrics including transaction volume, network activity, and market prices. It's useful for analysis of different blockchains, including Bitcoin and Ethereum.

DappRadar.com: It provides information and insights about decentralized applications (dApps) on various blockchain platforms, including those that power NFT marketplaces and games. It's a valuable tool for tracking dApp usage, transaction volume, and related NFT activity.

NFTStats.com: NFTStats provides detailed data and analytics on the NFT market, offering insights into different collections, marketplaces, and individual tokens. It's an excellent resource for tracking trends, price changes, and trading volume in the NFT space.

Avoiding Common Pitfalls of Investing in
Cryptocurrencies and NFTs

The burgeoning worlds of cryptocurrencies and non-fungible tokens (NFTs) offer investors a wealth of opportunities in the digital empire. However, as with any form of investment, these opportunities are accompanied by risks and potential pitfalls.

Cryptocurrency investments are often associated with the risk of fraudulent activities and scams. Investors must be vigilant in their research, selecting only reputable platforms and services for their transactions. Utilize well-established exchanges, such as Coinbase, Binance, or Kraken, and employ secure storage solutions like hardware wallets to protect your digital assets. Furthermore, pay close attention to projects that display signs of a pump-and-dump scheme, where prices are artificially inflated only to be sold off quickly, leaving investors at a loss.

The volatile nature of the cryptocurrency market can also create a sense of urgency, driving investors to make impulsive decisions. To counteract this, cultivate patience and develop a solid, long-term investment strategy. This approach can help mitigate the risks associated with short-term market fluctuations, providing a more stable foundation for success in the digital asset space.

In the jurisdiction of NFTs, the potential for fraud is equally present. Scammers may create counterfeit or unauthorized NFTs, capitalizing on the enthusiasm of unsuspecting investors. To avoid this trap, verify the provenance and authenticity of NFTs through trusted platforms, such as OpenSea, Rarible, or SuperRare. Additionally, engage in due diligence by researching the creator's reputation and the NFT's utility within its respective ecosystem.

Another pitfall in the NFT market is overvaluing digital assets based on hype and speculation. To counter this, adopt a disciplined approach to valuation, considering factors such as rarity, utility, and the credibility of the creators. Also, maintain a diverse portfolio by investing in a variety of NFTs, spreading your risk across different sectors, and themes.

Summary

In the dynamic world of digital assets, where cryptocurrencies and NFTs coexist, it's essential to find a balance between the potential rewards and the inherent risks. This journey calls for a calculated approach, a comprehensive understanding of the constantly changing landscape, and a steadfast commitment to due diligence.

As we conclude this chapter, remember that the key to success in this complex domain lies in the perfect blend of caution and enthusiasm.

Part IV

Advanced Investment Strategies

Chapter 14

Introduction to Derivatives

Derivatives, those inscrutable financial instruments, trace their value to underlying assets such as stocks, bonds, currencies, commodities, or indices. Like a pendulum, they sway between speculation on future price movements and hedging against potential fluctuations.

These contracts, agreed upon by two parties, delineate the terms of a future transaction with the value derived from the underlying asset or commodity. In a choreographed exchange of cash flows, they dance to the rhythm of the asset's performance. Derivatives pirouette through exchanges or over-the-counter (OTC) dealings among financial institutions and sizable investors.

Their allure lies in the ability to hedge against risk, generate income through speculation, enhance market liquidity, and tailor contracts to suit the parties' desires. However, they are not without peril. Complexity shrouds derivatives, often challenging the comprehension of investors. Highly leveraged, they may yield considerable gains or losses from minute shifts in the underlying asset.

These instruments face the specter of counterparty risk, as one participant may falter in fulfilling its obligations. Market risk lingers, as changing conditions sway the derivative's value, and regulatory risk looms, with potential alterations in requirements that could affect their worth. Nevertheless, derivatives persist as a captivating dance between opportunity and risk, gracefully unfolding in the world of finance.

Types of Derivatives

Forward Contracts: Customized contracts for purchasing or selling assets at preordained prices on future dates, tailored to the parties' desires and eschewing exchange trading.

Futures Contracts: Standardized, exchange-traded agreements for transacting assets at predetermined prices on specified future dates, exuding liquidity.

Options: Contracts bestowing rights without obligations to buy or sell assets at pre-set prices on or before specified dates. Diverging into call options (long) for buying and put options (short) for selling, with myriad strategies to unveil later in this chapter.

Swaps: Contracts binding two parties to exchange distinct cash flows over a designated period, encompassing interest rate swaps, currency swaps, and commodity swaps.

Credit Derivatives: Instruments for transferring credit risk, such as credit default swaps for bond default risk transfer, and credit-linked notes tethered to borrowers' creditworthiness.

Structured Finance Products: Intricate instruments born from fusing derivatives and other financial instruments to achieve specific risk/return profiles, including collateralized debt obligations (CDOs) and mortgage-backed securities (MBS).

Energy Derivatives: Instruments for hedging against price fluctuations in energy commodities, such as crude oil, natural gas, and electricity.

Metal Derivatives: Instruments for mitigating price fluctuations in metal commodities, including gold, silver, and copper.

Real Estate Derivatives: Instruments for shielding against price fluctuations in real estate assets, encompassing commercial and residential properties.

Emission Derivatives: Instruments for hedging against variations in the cost of emission reduction compliance, including emission allowances, futures, and options.

Cryptocurrency Derivatives: Instruments grounded in cryptocurrency values, such as Bitcoin or Ethereum.

Volatility Derivatives: Instruments for hedging against underlying asset price fluctuations, centered on volatility rather than price, with examples such as variance swaps and volatility futures.

Inflation Derivatives: Instruments for safeguarding against inflation rate changes, including inflation swaps and inflation-linked bonds.

FX Derivatives: Instruments for insulating against exchange rate fluctuations between currencies, comprising currency futures, options, and swaps.

This realm of derivatives, rich and varied, is but a glimpse into the world's vast financial markets. As we venture deeper, we shall explore futures and options in the subsequent chapters, unearthing their intricacies and illuminating their potential.

Chapter 15

Futures

Futures, an integral component of the financial markets, are standardized, legally binding agreements between two parties to buy or sell a specific asset at a predetermined price on a specified future date. These contracts are traded on centralized exchanges, ensuring transparency, liquidity, and efficient price discovery.

Designed to cater to various asset classes, futures contracts can be based on physical commodities, financial instruments, or indices. Market participants, such as hedgers and speculators, use futures for diverse purposes like mitigating price risks, capitalizing on market fluctuations, or enhancing portfolio diversification.

Given the leverage and potential volatility involved, it is essential for investors and traders to exercise caution, thoroughly assess their risk tolerance, and employ robust risk management strategies when engaging in futures trading.

Pivotal aspects of futures to bear in mind:

- A futures contract is a legally binding accord to transact a specific asset at a predetermined price on a future date.

- The asset underlying a futures contract can be a tangible commodity, such as wheat or oil, or a financial instrument, such as a currency or bond.

- Futures contracts are exchanged within futures exchanges, serving as a central marketplace for buyers and sellers to convene and trade.

- The price of a futures contract is forged by market supply and demand forces, influenced by factors including the underlying asset's price, economic conditions, and governmental policies.

- Futures contracts possess standardized terms, including the underlying asset, asset quantity, delivery date, and minimum price fluctuations (tick size).

- Futures market participants span speculators, who trade contracts for profit, and hedgers, who employ contracts to mitigate the risk of price fluctuations in the underlying asset.

- Trading futures entails substantial risk, as contract prices may oscillate dramatically due to shifts in the underlying asset's price and other factors. Consequently, traders and investors must carefully evaluate their risk tolerance.

Types of Futures

Futures contracts, diverse in nature, cater to various asset classes and industries:

Physical delivery futures: These contracts necessitate the buyer's acquisition of the underlying asset upon expiration. For instance, a live cattle contract may be used by a rancher to lock in a price for their cattle, while the buyer may hedge against potential price increases or speculate on future cattle prices.

Cash-settled futures: Unlike physical delivery futures, these contracts require cash settlement between the buyer and seller upon expiration. A stock index contract is a prime example of a cash-settled futures contract.

Agricultural futures: These contracts facilitate the trading of agricultural commodities, such as wheat, corn, and soybeans. A corn contract, for example, obligates the buyer to purchase a specified quantity of corn at a predetermined price upon expiration.

Financial futures: Designed for trading financial instruments like currencies, interest rates, and stock indices, financial futures exemplify the versatility of futures contracts. A Euro/US Dollar (EUR/USD) currency pair contract serves as a case in point.

Index futures: These contracts involve trading a basket of underlying assets, such as a stock or commodity index. The S&P 500 index contract is an example of index futures.

Energy futures: Energy futures contracts facilitate trading in energy commodities like crude oil, natural gas, and heating oil. A West Texas Intermediate (WTI) crude oil contract exemplifies this type of futures contract.

Metals futures: Metals futures contracts cater to metallic commodities, such as gold, silver, and copper. A gold contract, for example, obligates the buyer to purchase a specific gold quantity at a predetermined price upon expiration.

Emissions futures: These contracts focus on trading greenhouse gas emission allowances, such as carbon dioxide. A carbon dioxide allowance contract is a prime example of emissions futures.

Weather futures: Weather futures contracts deal with weather-related variables like temperature and precipitation. A temperature contract, for instance, obligates the buyer to purchase a specific quantity of degrees at a predetermined price upon expiration.

Real estate futures: Real estate futures contracts involve trading real estate properties or indices. For example, a specific property contract would obligate the buyer to purchase the property at a predetermined price upon expiration.

How to choose Futures

- **Scrutinize the underlying asset**: To make an informed choice, carefully examine the underlying asset of a futures contract, as its price is shaped by the supply and demand dynamics of that asset. Scrutinize market conditions, price trends, and the risk profile to gain a comprehensive understanding. For example, when considering a gold futures contract, investigate gold production, demand from various industries, and historical price fluctuations.

- **Ascertain the trade's purpose**: Determine whether the trade is intended for speculation or risk management. Speculators seek profits from price movements, while hedgers aim to mitigate the risk of price fluctuations in the underlying asset. For instance, a speculator might trade crude oil futures to capitalize on expected price changes, while an airline company may use futures to hedge against potential fuel price increases.

- **Assess the expiration date**: The expiration date of a futures contract signals its end, culminating in the delivery of the underlying asset (for physical delivery contracts) or a cash settlement (for cash-settled contracts). Select a contract with an expiration date that aligns with your desired timeframe for the trade, be it short-term, medium-term, or long-term.

- **Evaluate margin requirements**: Futures contracts necessitate maintaining a minimum amount of collateral, known as margin, in traders' accounts to cover potential losses. Examine the margin requirements of a contract before entering into it, as higher margin requirements could tie up more of your capital and affect your trading flexibility.

- **Opt for a reputable exchange**: Choosing a reputable futures exchange is crucial, as it serves as the central marketplace for buyers and sellers to trade. Open an account with a broker or trading platform that offers access to futures markets, such as Interactive Brokers, TD Ameritrade, or Fidelity. Seek exchanges with robust regulatory oversight, transparent pricing, and efficient trade execution, like the Chicago Mercantile Exchange (CME) or the Intercontinental Exchange (ICE).

- **Factor in the costs**: Trading costs, encompassing fees and commissions, can influence the overall profitability of a futures trade. Compare the costs of various exchanges and brokers to pinpoint the most cost-effective option. Additionally, consider other potential costs, such as data fees, platform fees, or account maintenance fees, to ensure a comprehensive assessment.

Examples:

Hedging in agricultural commodities: A farmer growing corn anticipates that corn prices may decline before harvest, potentially affecting their income. To hedge against this risk, the farmer can sell corn futures contracts at the current market price. By doing this, they effectively lock in a guaranteed selling price for their corn, mitigating potential financial losses if the market price declines. This expert-level strategy is commonly employed by agricultural producers to manage price risk. A reputable resource to study and monitor agricultural commodity futures would be the U.S. Department of Agriculture (USDA) website and the Chicago Mercantile Exchange (CME) Group's agricultural futures market data.

Speculating in currency futures: A currency trader believes that the Euro will appreciate against the U.S. Dollar in the coming months due to a more robust economic outlook in the Eurozone. To capitalize on this potential price movement, the trader buys Euro/US Dollar (EUR/USD) futures contracts. If the Euro indeed appreciates, the trader can profit from the increase in the currency pair's value. Forex traders often utilize expert analysis from resources such as DailyFX, Investing.com, or ForexFactory for insights into currency markets and potential trading opportunities.

Hedging in the energy market: An airline company expects crude oil prices to rise in the near future, which would increase fuel costs and negatively impact their profits. To hedge against this risk, the company can buy crude oil futures contracts at the current market price, locking in the cost of fuel for a specified period. In doing so, they protect themselves against potential increases in fuel costs. The Energy Information Administration (EIA) and the Intercontinental Exchange (ICE) offer valuable data and resources for understanding the dynamics of the energy market.

Diversifying a portfolio with index futures: An investor with a stock-heavy portfolio wants to hedge against potential market downturns while maintaining exposure to potential market gains. They decide to use index futures, such as the S&P 500 E-mini futures contracts, to achieve this balance. By strategically buying and selling index futures in conjunction with their existing stock positions, the investor can hedge against market volatility and manage risk more effectively. To stay informed on market trends and index futures, investors can turn to resources like Yahoo

Finance, CNBC, or Bloomberg for expert analysis and data.

Useful resources to analyze futures

CME Group: The Chicago Mercantile Exchange (CME Group) is the world's leading and most diverse derivatives marketplace. It provides futures and options on futures for a range of asset classes. Their website offers educational materials, market data, and trading tools that can be helpful for futures traders.

Commitment of Traders Report: The Commodity Futures Trading Commission (CFTC) provides a weekly report called the Commitment of Traders Report. It details the holdings of various types of traders in the futures market, offering valuable insights about market sentiment.

Barchart.com: Barchart is a leading provider of financial content, including futures prices for commodities, equities, indices, and currencies. The site offers comprehensive futures data, charts, news, and tools for technical analysis, making it a great resource for futures traders.

TradingView.com: TradingView is a social network for traders and investors. It offers a wide range of features, including real-time futures charts for a variety of asset classes, technical analysis tools, and a futures screener tool. Users can also share their trading ideas and strategies with the community.

Summary

In the vast landscape of financial markets, futures contracts stand as pivotal elements, meticulously designed to span a diverse range of assets. These legally binding agreements, blending speculation and hedging, harmonize the present with the future, guiding traders and investors through the intricate dynamics of risk and reward. As market participants navigate the ever-changing terrain, futures provide an opportunity to embark on this journey with a balance of caution and determination.

The futures market, a complex fabric interwoven with threads of commodities, financial instruments, and indices, extends its reach to incorporate the aspirations and endeavors of its many participants. Amidst the nuances of expiration dates, margin requirements, and price fluctuations, the futures market casts its allure, inviting the prudent and the bold to explore the depths of uncertainty with skill and modishness. For those who accept its invitation, the futures market unfurls its sails, charting a course through the winds of change with the promise of adventure and discovery.

Chapter 16

Options

Investing is a voyage into the unknown, a journey fraught with excitement, risk, and potential reward. As we navigate the ever-changing waters of the markets, we seek out tools and strategies to help us navigate the tides and chart our course to success. And in this quest, there are few tools more powerful or fascinating than options.

Options are like the stars in the sky, twinkling and dancing with the ebb and flow of market forces. They offer a unique way to harness the volatility and unpredictability of the markets, granting investors the power to profit even when traditional investment strategies fail. But like the stars, options are also complex and mysterious, their inner workings shrouded in the darkness of financial jargon and esoteric concepts.

In this section, we will embark on a journey of discovery, peering into the hidden depths of the options universe and uncovering its many secrets. We will explore the fundamental principles of options trading, unlocking the secrets of calls and puts, premiums and strike prices, to the more advanced strategies of covered calls and straddles, we will delve deep into the heart of options trading. And we will venture beyond the basics, exploring the myriad ways in which options can be used to manage risk, generate income, and enhance overall returns.

Fundamental components of options

At its core, an option is a financial contract that gives the holder the right, but not the obligation, to buy or sell an underlying asset at a specified price within a specified time frame.

Strike Price: The strike price is one of the key components of an option contract. It represents the price at which the underlying asset can be bought or sold if the option is exercised.

> For call options, the strike price is the price at which the underlying asset can be purchased, while for put options, the strike price is the price at which the underlying asset can be sold. The strike price is a vital factor in determining the potential profit or loss of an options trade.

Expiration Date: The expiration date is another critical component of an option contract. It represents the date on which the option contract expires. If the option is not exercised by this date, it becomes worthless. Generally, options have expiration dates ranging from a few days to several years. The expiration date is a crucial factor to consider when trading options since it sets a strict time frame within which the option must be exercised.

Premium: The premium is the price that the option buyer pays to the option seller for the right to buy or sell the underlying asset. The premium is determined by a number of factors, including the current price of the underlying asset, the strike price, the time until expiration, and the volatility of the underlying asset. The premium is the price that the option buyer must pay for the right to potentially profit from the price movement of the underlying asset.

Intrinsic Value: Intrinsic value is the value of an option that is in-the-money, which means that the option has a positive payoff if it were to be exercised immediately. For call options, the intrinsic value is the difference between the underlying asset's current price and the strike price. For put options, the intrinsic value is the difference between the strike price and the underlying asset's current price.

Time Value: Time value is the portion of an option's premium that is attributable to the amount of time remaining until the option's expiration date. It reflects the amount of time that the underlying asset has to move in the direction that the option buyer is anticipating. As the expiration date approaches, the time value of an option decreases, which is also known as time decay.

Implied Volatility: Implied Volatility is a measure of the amount by which the price of an underlying asset is expected to fluctuate over a given period. Higher volatility typically results in a higher option premium since there is a greater likelihood of the underlying asset experiencing significant price movements.

Leverage: Options provide traders with leverage, which means that a relatively small investment can control a much larger amount of an underlying asset. This can result in both significant profits and losses, depending on the success of the options trade.

Overall, grasping these fundamental components of options is crucial for successful options trading. Traders must carefully consider each component when evaluating potential options trades, in order to effectively manage risk and maximize profit potential.

Option Greeks

- The options greeks are a set of variables that are used to measure the sensitivity of the price of an option to various factors that can affect it.

- These factors include the underlying asset's price, time to expiration, volatility, and interest rates.

Options greeks comprise:

1. **Delta (Δ)**: Delta is an Option Greek that measures the sensitivity of an option's price to changes in the price of the underlying asset. Delta is expressed as a number between 0 and 1, where a delta of 1 means that the option's price will increase by $1 for every $1 increase in the price of the underlying asset. For example, if an investor owns a call option with a delta of 0.6 and the price of the underlying asset rises by $1, the option's price will increase by $0.60.

2. **Gamma (Γ)**: Gamma is another Option Greek that measures the rate of change of an option's delta in response to changes in the price of the underlying asset. A high gamma means that the delta of the option will change rapidly in response

to changes in the price of the underlying asset. This can be advantageous for investors who are looking to profit from short-term price movements in the underlying asset. For example, if an investor owns a call option with a high gamma and the price of the underlying asset rises rapidly, the option's delta will increase quickly, potentially resulting in a substantial profit.

3. **Theta (Θ)**: Theta is an Option Greek that measures the rate of time decay of an option's price. As an option approaches its expiration date, its time value decreases, and its price can decrease as well. Theta measures the rate of this time decay. This means that as the expiration date of an option approaches, its value will decrease over time. For example, if an investor owns a call option with a theta of -0.05 and the option has 30 days left until expiration, the option's price will decrease by $0.05 per day due to time decay.

4. **Vega (v)**: Vega is an Option Greek that measures the sensitivity of an option's price to changes in implied volatility. Implied volatility is a measure of the market's expectation of the future volatility of the underlying asset. A high vega means that the option's price will increase in response to increases in implied volatility. This means that when implied volatility is high, options prices will be higher, as the market is expecting larger price movements in the underlying asset. For example, if an investor owns a call option with a vega of 0.10 and the implied volatility of the underlying asset increases by 1%, the option's price will increase by $0.10.

5. **Rho (ρ)**: Measures the sensitivity of the option's price to changes in the interest rate. When interest rates rise, the value of call options typically increases, while the value of put options typically decreases, and vice versa. This is because higher interest rates increase the cost of borrowing money, which can lead to lower demand for stocks and other assets. As a result, the value of call options can increase as investors look for ways to limit their exposure to the market.

Example:

Suppose an investor buys a call option on 100 shares of XYZ Company with a strike price of $50 and an expiration date of 6 months from now. The investor pays a premium for the option, let's say $2 per share, or $200 total. The delta of the option is 0.60, meaning that for every $1 increase in the price of XYZ Company's shares, the option's price will increase by $0.60.

Suppose that 3 months into the option's lifespan, the price of XYZ Company's shares rises to $55. At this point, the delta of the option has increased to 0.80, meaning that for every $1 increase in the price of XYZ Company's shares, the option's price will increase by $0.80.

Option greeks are useful for option traders and investors because they allow them to understand the risks and potential rewards of their positions, and to make informed decisions about how to manage those positions. They also allow traders and investors to construct complex option strategies, such as spreads and combinations, that can help to mitigate risk and capture specific market conditions.

The Options Industry Council, the Chicago Board Options Exchange (CBOE), and Investopedia are excellent resources for options trading education.

Call options

Call options provide investors with an opportunity to potentially profit from upward price movements in the underlying asset. By purchasing a call option, an investor acquires the right, but not the obligation, to buy the underlying asset at a predetermined price (strike price) at a specific time in the future (expiration date).

Example: For instance, imagine a seasoned financial trader Sarah who believes that the price of XYZ Company's stock will rise in the next month due to positive earnings reports. Sarah buys a call option on XYZ Company's stock with a strike price of $50 and an expiration date of six months from now. In exchange for this right, Sarah pays a premium of $2 per share, amounting to $200 for the entire option (100 shares x $2/share).

One month later, Sarah's forecast proves correct, as the price of XYZ Company's stock increases to $55 per share. She then exercises her option and purchases 100 shares of XYZ Company's stock at the strike price of $50 per share. Sarah subsequently sells the stock for $55 per share, earning a profit of $500 (100 shares x $5/share).

Alternatively, Sarah could choose to sell the option without exercising it. Suppose the price of the stock increases to $60, and the premium increases to $6. In that case, her profit would be $400 (100 shares x $6/share minus initial $200 premium). However, if the price of the stock had not increased above the strike price, Sarah would have let the option expire, thereby avoiding the obligation to buy the stock. In that scenario, she would have lost the $200 premium that she paid for the option or sold the option for a loss without losing the entire premium.

Put options

Put options can be used by investors to potentially profit from downward price movements in the underlying asset. With a put option, the holder has the right, but not the obligation, to sell the underlying asset at a predetermined price at a specific time in the future.

Example: Consider a financial trader Maria who believes that the price of DEF Company's stock will decrease in the next month due to negative earnings reports. Maria buys a put option on DEF Company's stock with a strike price of $60 and an expiration date of one month from now. She pays a premium of $3 per share, which amounts to $300 for the entire option (100 shares x $3/share).

One month later, the price of DEF Company's stock has indeed decreased to $55 per share. Maria exercises her option and sells 100 shares of DEF Company's stock at the strike price of $60 per share, receiving $6,000 for the stock (100 shares x $60/share).

Alternatively, Maria could choose to sell the option without exercising it and profit on the increased premium. Suppose the price of the stock had not decreased below the strike price. In that case, Maria would have let the option expire and would not have had to sell the stock. She would have lost the premium of $300 that she paid for the option, or sold the option for a loss without losing the entire premium.

Options Strategies

Options trading offers a plethora of strategies that traders can utilize to gain a favorable outcome. Each strategy comes with its own unique risk-reward characteristics, and selecting the right strategy is crucial to maximize potential profits while minimizing risks.

Basic Options Strategies:

- The **Long Call** is a bullish strategy, involving the purchase of a call option with the expectation that the underlying asset's price will rise above the strike price. For example, consider purchasing an AAPL long call option with a strike price of $150. As the stock price ascends, the value of the option increases, generating potential profit.

  Example: Suppose AAPL is currently trading at $145. You believe the stock price will rise in the near future, and you decide to buy a call option.

  a. Identify the option: Choose an AAPL call option with a strike price of $150 and an expiration date one month away.

b. Calculate the premium: The option premium is $5 per share. Since each option contract represents 100 shares, the cost to purchase one contract is $500 ($5 * 100 shares).

c. Execute the trade: Buy the call option at the $5 premium.

d. Monitor the position: If AAPL's price rises above $155 ($150 strike price + $5 premium), you'll be in a profitable position. You can either exercise the option to buy 100 shares at $150 or sell the option for a profit before the expiration date.

- The **Long Put** is a bearish strategy that entails buying a put option with the anticipation that the underlying asset's price will fall below the strike price. Imagine a MSFT long put option with a strike price of $200. As the stock price declines, the investor benefits from the drop in value.

Example: Suppose MSFT is trading at $210, and you believe the stock price will decline. You decide to buy a put option.

a. Identify the option: Choose an MSFT put option with a strike price of $200 and an expiration date one month away.

b. Calculate the premium: The option premium is $3 per share. The cost to purchase one contract is $300 ($3 * 100 shares).

c. Execute the trade: Buy the put option at the $3 premium.

d. Monitor the position: If MSFT's price falls below $197 ($200 strike price - $3 premium), you'll be in a profitable position. You can either exercise the option to sell 100 shares at

$200 or sell the option for a profit before the expiration date.

- The **Covered Call** is a conservative strategy that generates income while relinquishing potential gains above the strike price. By owning the underlying asset and selling a call option against it, the investor establishes a consistent income stream. Picture a TSLA investor who owns 100 shares and sells a covered call with a strike price of $800. The investor benefits from the premium received but foregoes any gains beyond the strike price. It's essential to mention that, the investor owns 100 shares of the underlying asset (TSLA) for each call option sold since one options contract typically corresponds to 100 shares.

    Example: Suppose you own 100 shares of TSLA, currently trading at $750. You want to generate income from your holdings without selling the shares. You decide to sell a covered call option.

    a. Identify the option: Choose a TSLA call option with a strike price of $800 and an expiration date one month away.
    b. Calculate the premium: The option premium is $10 per share. The income you receive for selling one contract is $1,000 ($10 * 100 shares).
    c. Execute the trade: Sell the call option, receiving the $1,000 premium.
    d. Monitor the position: If TSLA's price remains below $800, the option will expire worthless, and you keep the premium. If TSLA's price rises above $800, you may have to sell your

100 shares at the strike price, forfeiting potential gains beyond $800.

- The **Protective Put** is a risk management strategy in which an investor purchases a put option to protect an existing long position in the underlying asset. This approach serves as an insurance policy, limiting potential losses. Consider an AMZN investor purchasing a protective put option with a strike price of $3,000. Should the stock price fall below the strike price, the investor's losses are limited.

Example: Suppose you own 100 shares of AMZN, currently trading at $3,100. You want to protect your investment from potential losses. You decide to buy a protective put option.

a. Identify the option: Choose an AMZN put option with a strike price of $3,000 and an expiration date one month away.
b. Calculate the premium: The option premium is $30 per share. The cost to purchase one contract is $3,000 ($30 * 100 shares).
c. Execute the trade: Buy the put option at the $30 premium.
d. Monitor the position: If AMZN's price falls below $3,000, your protective put limits your losses, as you have the right to sell your shares at the $3,000 strike price. If AMZN's price stays above $3,000, the option will expire worthless, and your cost is the $3,000 premium.

Advanced Options Strategies

- **Vertical Spreads** employ a combination of options with different strike prices, allowing investors to capitalize on various market conditions. The **Bull Call Spread**, for example, involves purchasing a call option with a lower strike price while simultaneously selling a call option with a higher strike price. This strategy is employed when an investor expects a moderate increase in the underlying asset's price. Conversely, the **Bear Put Spread** is executed by purchasing a put option with a higher strike price and selling a put option with a lower strike price, catering to investors who anticipate a moderate decrease in the underlying asset's price.

Examples:

Bull Call Spread: Suppose NFLX is trading at $500, and you expect a moderate increase in the stock price. You decide to initiate a bull call spread.

a. Identify the options: Choose a NFLX call option with a strike price of $500 (lower strike) and another call option with a strike price of $520 (higher strike), both with the same expiration date.
b. Calculate the premiums: The $500 call option premium is $15, and the $520 call option premium is $8.
c. Execute the trade: Buy the $500 call option for $15 and simultaneously sell the $520 call option for $8.
d. Monitor the position: The maximum profit occurs if NFLX's price is at or above $520 at expiration, which is equal to $7 ($20

difference in strike prices - $13 net premium). The maximum loss is the net premium of $13, which occurs if the stock price remains at or below $500.

Bear Put Spread: Suppose GOOGL is trading at $2,400, and you expect a moderate decrease in the stock price. You decide to initiate a bear put spread.

a. Identify the options: Choose a GOOGL put option with a strike price of $2,400 (higher strike) and another put option with a strike price of $2,380 (lower strike), both with the same expiration date.
b. Calculate the premiums: The $2,400 put option premium is $30, and the $2,380 put option premium is $25.
c. Execute the trade: Buy the $2,400 put option for $30 and simultaneously sell the $2,380 put option for $25.
d. Monitor the position: The maximum profit occurs if GOOGL's price is at or below $2,380 at expiration, which is equal to $15 ($20 difference in strike prices - $5 net premium). The maximum loss is the net premium of $5, which occurs if the stock price remains at or above $2,400.

- **Iron Condor:** The Iron Condor is a neutral options strategy designed to profit from low volatility in the underlying asset's price. By selling an out-of-the-money call and put while simultaneously purchasing a further out-of-the-money call and put, the investor establishes a profit range within which they can capitalize on the lack of movement in the underlying asset's price. The maximum profit is limited to the net credit received from selling the options (the premiums collected from selling the out-of-the-money call and put options minus the premiums paid for buying the further out-of-the-money call and put options). The maximum loss is limited to the difference between the strike prices of the call (or put) options minus the net credit received.

Example: Suppose IBM is trading at $140, and you expect low volatility in the stock price. You decide to initiate an iron condor.

a. Identify the options: Choose IBM call options with strike prices of $145 (lower call) and $150 (higher call), and put options with strike prices of $135 (higher put) and $130 (lower put), all with the same expiration date.
b. Calculate the premiums: The $145 call option premium is $4, the $150 call option premium is $2, the $135 put option premium is $3, and the $130 put option premium is $1.
c. Execute the trade: Sell the $145 call option for $4, buy the $150 call option for $2, sell the $135 put option for $3, and buy the $130 put option for $1.
d. Monitor the position: The maximum profit is equal to the net premium received, which is $4 in this case ($4 - $2 + $3 - $1). The maximum loss occurs if IBM's price is above $150 or below $130 at expiration, which is equal to the difference between strike prices minus the net premium, or $6 ($10 - $4).

- **Straddle and Strangle**: The Straddle and Strangle strategies cater to investors who expect significant price movements in the underlying asset but are unsure of the direction. Both strategies involve purchasing a call and put option, with the Straddle using the same strike price for both options and the Strangle using different strike prices. These strategies allow investors to profit from large price swings in either direction.

  Example: Suppose NVDA is trading at $200, and you expect a significant price movement but are unsure of the direction. You decide to initiate a straddle.

  a. Identify the options: Choose NVDA call and put options with the same strike price of $200 and the same expiration date.
  b. Calculate the premiums: The call option premium is $10, and the put option premium is $9.
  c. Execute the trade: Buy the call option for $10 and simultaneously buy the put option for $9.
  d. Monitor the position: The breakeven points occur when NVDA's price is at $191 ($200 - $9) or $210 ($200 + $10). The maximum profit is theoretically unlimited, as the stock price can rise indefinitely, while the maximum loss is the net premium paid, which is $19 ($10 + $9).

  For a strangle, simply choose call and put options with different strike prices (e.g., $190 for the put and $210 for the call). The breakeven points, maximum profit, and maximum loss calculations will be slightly different due to the change in strike prices.

- **Butterfly Spread**: The Butterfly Spread is a low-risk options strategy that profits from a limited range of price movement in the underlying asset. It involves purchasing a call option at a lower strike price, selling two call options at a middle strike price, and purchasing a call option at a higher strike price. This strategy creates a profit zone around the middle strike price, allowing the investor to capitalize on minimal price fluctuations.

  Example: Suppose FB is trading at $330, and you expect the stock price to remain within a limited range. You decide to initiate a butterfly spread.

  a. Identify the options: Choose FB call options with strike prices of $320 (lower strike), $330 (middle strike), and $340 (higher strike), all with the same expiration date.
  b. Calculate the premiums: The $320 call option premium is $18, the $330 call option premium is $10, and the $340 call option premium is $4.
  c. Execute the trade: Buy the $320 call option for $18, sell two $330 call options for $10 each, and buy the $340 call option for $4.
  d. Monitor the position: The maximum profit occurs when FB's price is at the $330 strike price at expiration, which is equal to the difference between the middle and lower strike prices minus the net premium, or $2 ($10 - $8). The maximum loss is the net premium paid, which is $8 ($18 - 2*$10 + $4).

- **Calendar Spread**: The Calendar Spread, also known as a horizontal spread, is an options strategy that profits from the passage of time and differences in implied volatility. By selling a short-term option and buying a longer-term option with the same strike price, an investor can take advantage of time decay and changes in implied volatility. This strategy is typically employed when an investor expects minimal price movement in the underlying asset over the short term, while anticipating a potentially larger move in the longer term.

  Example: Suppose BABA is trading at $220, and you expect time decay and implied volatility to work in your favor. You decide to initiate a calendar spread.

  a. Identify the options: Choose a BABA call option with a strike price of $225 and expiration dates one month apart (e.g., short-term option expiring in one month and long-term option expiring in two months).
  b. Calculate the premiums: The short-term call option premium is $5, and the long-term call option premium is $9.
  c. Execute the trade: Sell the short-term $225 call option for $5 and simultaneously buy the long-term $225 call option for $9.
  d. Monitor the position: The maximum profit occurs when BABA's price is at the $225 strike price at the short-term option's expiration date, as the short-term option expires worthless and the long-term option retains its value. The maximum loss is equal to the net premium paid, which is $4 ($9 - $5).

- **Ratio Spread**: A Ratio Spread is an options strategy that involves buying and selling an unequal number of options contracts on the same underlying asset with the same expiration date. This strategy allows investors to capitalize on different market conditions and manage risk.

  For example, a Call Ratio Spread involves buying one call option with a lower strike price while simultaneously selling two or more call options with a higher strike price. This strategy is employed when an investor expects a moderate increase in the underlying asset's price but wants to limit the downside risk. Conversely, a Put Ratio Spread is executed by buying one put option with a higher strike price and selling two or more put options with a lower strike price, catering to investors who anticipate a moderate decrease in the underlying asset's price but also want to limit their risk exposure.

  Example: Suppose XOM is trading at $80, and you expect a moderate increase in the stock price. You decide to initiate a call ratio spread.

  a. Identify the options: Choose XOM call options with strike prices of $82 (lower strike) and $84 (higher strike), both with the same expiration date.
  b. Calculate the premiums: The $82 call option premium is $3, and the $84 call option premium is $1.
  c. Execute the trade: Buy one $82 call option for $3 and simultaneously sell two $84 call options for $1 each.

d. Monitor the position: The maximum profit occurs when XOM's price is at the $84 strike price at expiration, which is equal to the difference between the strike prices minus the net premium, or $1 ($2 - $1). The maximum loss is the net premium paid, which is $1 ($3 - 2*$1).

- **Diagonal Spread**: A Diagonal Spread is an options strategy that combines options with different strike prices and expiration dates, allowing investors to capitalize on changes in implied volatility and time decay. This strategy is a variation of a vertical spread but with differing expiration dates, resulting in a "diagonal" relationship between the options.

  For example, a Call Diagonal Spread involves selling a call option with a lower strike price and a near-term expiration date while simultaneously buying a call option with a higher strike price and a longer-term expiration date. This strategy is employed when an investor expects a gradual increase in the underlying asset's price over time and wants to benefit from the time decay of the near-term option. Conversely, a Put Diagonal Spread is executed by selling a put option with a higher strike price and a near-term expiration date and buying a put option with a lower strike price and a longer-term expiration date, catering to investors who anticipate a gradual decrease in the underlying asset's price while benefiting from time decay.

  Example: Suppose V is trading at $220, and you want to take advantage of time decay and changes in implied volatility. You decide to initiate a diagonal spread.

a. Identify the options: Choose a V call option with a strike price of $230 and a near-term expiration date (e.g., one month away) and another call option with the same strike price and a longer-term expiration date (e.g., three months away).

b. Calculate the premiums: The near-term call option premium is $7, and the longer-term call option premium is $12.

c. Execute the trade: Sell the near-term $230 call option for $7 and simultaneously buy the longer-term $230 call option for $12.

d. Monitor the position: The maximum profit potential is theoretically unlimited as the longer-term option could increase in value if the underlying asset's price continues to rise significantly. However, the maximum loss is equal to the net premium paid, which is $5 ($12 - $7).

- **Naked Call and Naked Put:** The Naked Call and Naked Put strategies exemplify uncovered options strategies, wherein investors sell options without holding a corresponding position in the underlying asset. While these strategies can generate income from option premiums, they expose investors to potentially **unlimited risk**.

  o The **Naked Call** strategy involves selling a call option without owning the underlying asset. Investors employing this strategy anticipate that the price of the underlying asset will not exceed the option's strike price, allowing them to retain the premium received. However, should the asset's price rise above the strike price, the investor may face unlimited losses, as they are obligated to deliver the shares at the strike price.

Example: Assume XYZ stock is trading at $50, and you believe that its price will not increase significantly in the near future. You decide to sell a naked call option.

a. Choose an XYZ call option with a strike price of $55 and an expiration date one month away.
b. Calculate the premium: The call option premium is $2.
c. Execute the trade: Sell the $55 call option for $2.
d. Monitor the position: If XYZ's price remains below the $55 strike price at the option's expiration date, the option expires worthless, and you retain the $2 premium. However, if the price rises above $55, you face potentially unlimited losses, as you are obligated to provide the shares at $55, even if you have to buy them at a higher market price to fulfill your obligation.

o The **Naked Put** strategy entails selling a put option without holding a short position in the underlying asset. Investors adopting this strategy expect the asset's price to remain above the strike price, enabling them to collect the premium. Nevertheless, if the price declines below the strike price, the investor may incur substantial losses, as they are obliged to purchase the shares at the strike price.

Example: Suppose ABC stock is trading at $100, and you believe that its price will not decline significantly in the near future. You decide to sell a naked put option.

a. Choose an ABC put option with a strike price of $95 and an expiration date one month away.
b. Calculate the premium: The put option premium is $3.
c. Execute the trade: Sell the $95 put option for $3.
d. Monitor the position: If ABC's price remains above the $95 strike price at the option's expiration date, the option expires worthless, and you retain the $3 premium. However, if the price falls below $95, you may incur significant losses, as you are obligated to purchase the shares at $95, even if the current market price is lower.

The examples elucidated herein serve solely as educational illustrations. In practice, trading conditions, premiums, and the potential for profits or losses can fluctuate, contingent upon the particular options, underlying assets, and prevailing market circumstances.

By skillfully amalgamating these strategies and fine-tuning strike prices, expiration dates, and the number of options contracts, you can tailor bespoke strategies that align with your distinct market perspective and risk tolerance. It is imperative to bear in mind that options trading inherently entails risk; thus, comprehending the potential rewards and risks of each strategy is vital prior to embarking on any trade.

Risk Management & Strategy Selection in Options Trading

Navigating the complex protectorate of options trading with confidence and finesse requires the mastery of several key principles: determining risk tolerance, aligning strategies with market outlook, practicing appropriate position sizing, diversifying, and devising a well-defined exit strategy.

1. **Risk tolerance**: Each investor possesses a unique threshold for risk, which must be factored into the selection of options strategies. Striking a balance between potential rewards and acceptable risk is vital for a prosperous investment approach.

2. **Market outlook**: An investor's market perspective profoundly influences their choice of options strategies. Discerning the market's direction—whether bullish, bearish, or neutral— and opting for a suitable strategy is crucial for success.

3. **Position sizing**: Investors ought to determine their options positions' size based on their risk tolerance and overall portfolio. Proper position sizing aids in managing risk and maintaining a balanced investment approach.

4. **Diversification**: Spreading investments across various options strategies and underlying assets helps reduce overall portfolio risk. Diversification mitigates the impact of adverse market

movements by investing in multiple strategies and sectors.

5. **Exit strategy**: Crafting a lucid exit plan is an indispensable component of successful options trading. Knowing when to close or adjust a position, either to secure profits or curtail losses, is a vital skill for options traders.

Selecting Options with Precision

1. **Underlying asset**: Carefully consider the underlying asset of an option, as its price is influenced by the asset's supply and demand dynamics. Assess market conditions, price trends, and the risk profile of the asset.

2. **Trade purpose**: Determine whether the trade is speculative or for risk management. Speculators aim for profits from price movements, while hedgers seek to alleviate the risk of price fluctuations in the underlying asset.

3. **Expiration date**: Align the option's expiration date with the desired time frame for the trade, as it determines when the option expires and can no longer be exercised.

4. **Option type**: Choose between call options and put options based on the desired trade strategy.

5. **Reputable exchange**: Opt for a reputable options exchange that boasts robust regulatory oversight, transparent pricing, and efficient trade execution.

6. **Costs**: Trade costs, including fees and commissions, can impact the overall profitability of an options trade. Compare the costs of different exchanges and brokers to find the most cost-effective solution.

Useful resources to analyze Options

CBOE.com: The Chicago Board Options Exchange (CBOE) offers an extensive suite of educational materials about options trading, as well as a wide range of tools for analyzing and trading options. It also provides options market data, volatility indexes, and strategy performance metrics.

Quantcha.com: Quantcha is a suite of tools for searching, filtering, and analyzing stock options investments. It offers comprehensive coverage of the U.S. stock options market and includes sophisticated analytical tools, including scenario analysis, option strategy optimization, and risk management tools.

OptionsProfitCalculator.com: This online tool helps investors to calculate potential profit and loss scenarios for various options strategies. The platform provides clear, visual data and is easy to use, making it an ideal resource for beginners as well as experienced traders.

Summary

Options trading strategies present investors with a diverse palette of methods to harness market opportunities and adeptly manage risk. Ranging from the simplicity of buying and selling options to devising intricate spreads, each strategy encompasses its own unique blend of risks and rewards. Long call and long put options endow investors with the privilege to buy or sell an underlying asset at a predetermined price, while short call and short put options involve bestowing the right to buy or sell the asset at a designated price. Strategies such as covered calls and protective puts artfully merge options with a long position in the underlying asset, generating income or shielding against potential value depreciation. Spread strategies, like the elegant bull call and bear put spreads, gracefully limit potential losses while enabling investors to reap profits from fluctuations in the underlying asset's price. Furthermore, uncovered options strategies, such as Naked Call and Naked Put, exemplify audacious approaches that can yield income from option premiums at the expense of potentially boundless risk. Finally, sophisticated strategies like straddles and strangles encompass the acquisition of both call and put options to seize profits from significant shifts in the underlying asset, regardless of the direction.

To skillfully employ options strategies, investors must wield a deep comprehension of the market and the underlying asset, as well as devise a well-thought-out plan for managing risk. It is of utmost importance to carefully assess the risks and rewards of each strategy and establish a lucid exit plan for every trade. Traders should also remain vigilant of factors such as time decay and implied volatility on their options positions, refining their strategies as needed. By harnessing options strategies with finesse and a thorough understanding of the market landscape, investors can artfully optimize their profits while minimizing risks.

Chapter 17

Short Selling

Short selling, the artful maneuver of capitalizing on plummeting stock prices, represents a captivating yet contentious facet of the investment world. While initially appearing counterintuitive, this practice occupies a vital niche within finance, affording investors the chance to reap rewards in bearish markets and supplying a tempering force against unbridled enthusiasm.

As an investment tactic, short selling enables investors to derive profit from the depreciation in value of stocks, commodities, or other financial instruments. Fundamentally, it entails borrowing a security, vending it, and subsequently repurchasing it at a reduced rate to return to the lender, thus retaining the difference as earnings. This approach diverges from conventional investing, in which investors acquire at low prices and liquidate at higher ones to garner profits.

Mechanics of Short Selling

1. Borrowing the Security: To initiate the process, an investor (the short seller) liaises with their broker to orchestrate the borrowing of a security, typically procured from another investor's margin account. The broker delineates the terms of the

loan, encompassing interest rates and the stipulation of collateral to secure the transaction.

2. Selling the Security: Upon acquiring the borrowed security, the short seller proceeds to vend it within the open market, capitalizing on the prevailing market price and anticipating a subsequent decline in its value.

3. Buying Back the Security: Once the security's price diminishes, the short seller strategically repurchases it, ideally at a rate markedly lower than the original selling price. This maneuver is crucial to the success of the short-selling strategy, as it determines the potential profit margin.

4. Returning the Security: Lastly, the short seller fulfills their obligation by returning the borrowed security to the lender via the intermediary broker. In doing so, the investor retains the difference between the initial selling price and the subsequent repurchasing price, thus reaping the profits garnered through this sophisticated financial gambit.

Risks and Limitations

Short selling, despite its potential rewards, is accompanied by inherent risks. Given that a stock's capacity to appreciate is boundless, short sellers confront the daunting prospect of limitless losses. Furthermore, this practice necessitates borrowing expenses and margin prerequisites, which may constrain the investor's capacity to participate in alternative investment opportunities.

Additionally, short selling is subject to regulatory constraints and public scrutiny, which may impede the investor's ability to execute the strategy. Market conditions, liquidity, and the availability of shares to borrow can also impose limitations on short selling, making it a more challenging and potentially less viable option for some investors. In times of market turbulence, regulatory bodies may impose temporary restrictions on short selling, further complicating matters for those engaging in this practice.

Ultimately, while short selling presents a unique avenue for potentially realizing profits in declining markets, investors must weigh the risks and limitations against the potential rewards, ensuring that they possess a comprehensive understanding of the complexities involved before embarking on this intricate financial endeavor.

Types of Short Selling Strategies

Naked Short Selling: This audacious strategy entails short selling a security without first securing the borrowed shares or making arrangements to do so. As it can generate undue downward pressure on the security's price and potentially deplete the pool of shares available for borrowing, naked short selling is deemed illegal in most jurisdictions.

Covered Short Selling: A more conventional approach, covered short selling necessitates borrowing or arranging to borrow securities before selling them. By ensuring the availability of shares to be borrowed, this method minimizes risks for the seller and adheres to legal requirements.

Short Selling on Margin: Utilizing a margin account, this strategy enables sellers to borrow funds from their brokers to cover part or all of the cost of the securities being sold. Although this leveraging tactic can amplify potential profits or losses, it may prove enticing for those seeking higher returns on their short sales.

Short Selling Against the Box: A nuanced maneuver, this strategy involves a trader maintaining both long and short positions in the same security or related securities, intending to nullify the positions at a later date. This tactic can serve as a tax-deferral strategy, allowing traders to postpone realizing any gains or losses until the positions are closed.

Short Selling ETFs (Exchange Traded Funds): Representing investment vehicles that track the performance of specific indices or asset classes, ETFs can be traded like stocks. By short selling ETFs, traders can capitalize on the decline of the underlying assets tracked by these funds, expanding the opportunities for potential profit.

How to choose Short Selling Strategies

- **Know your goals**: Before engaging in any short selling strategy, it is essential to have a clear understanding of your objectives. Are you looking to capitalize on a decline in the price of a particular security or market? Are you using short selling as a hedging tool against potential losses in other investments? By defining your goals, you can make more informed decisions and avoid impulsive actions driven by emotions.

- **Understand the risks**: Short selling carries inherent risks that must be thoroughly comprehended. These risks include the potential for unlimited losses and increased market volatility. Understanding these risks and carefully selecting the appropriate strategies that align with your risk tolerance and investment objectives is critical to your success.

- **Consider the type of security**: Different securities have unique characteristics that may make them more or less suitable for short selling. Liquidity, volatility, and regulatory restrictions are just a few factors to consider. For instance, short selling highly liquid securities may be easier and more predictable, while short selling less liquid securities may carry additional risks.

- **Use stop-loss orders**: Utilizing stop-loss orders is a crucial technique to limit potential losses from short selling. It is a type of order that automatically closes out a short position if the price of the security reaches a specific level. This approach enables you to manage your risk by automatically triggering an exit from a trade, protecting you from any adverse effects of price movements.

- **Consider market conditions**: Short selling strategies can vary depending on the current market conditions. For example, in a bear market, where stocks are generally declining, short selling may be more attractive as there may be more opportunities to profit from declining prices. In a bull market, short selling may be riskier as the market is generally rising, and there may be fewer opportunities for profitable short selling.

- **Choose the right timing**: Timing is key in short selling. Choosing the right time to enter and exit a short position can make all the difference in achieving your investment goals. It is important to conduct thorough research and analysis to identify potential market trends and to use technical analysis tools to identify the optimal entry and exit points.

- **Select the appropriate short selling technique**: There are various short selling techniques that can be used, including shorting individual stocks, shorting market indices, and shorting exchange-traded funds (ETFs). Each technique carries its own risks and rewards, and it is important to select the appropriate technique based on your investment goals, risk tolerance, and market conditions.

- **Utilize short selling strategies**: There are several short selling strategies that can be used to mitigate risks and maximize profits. One such strategy is the short squeeze, which occurs when a heavily shorted stock rises sharply in price, forcing short sellers to cover their positions and resulting in further upward price momentum. Another strategy is the pairs trade, which involves simultaneously shorting one stock and going long on another stock in the same industry or sector.

- **Stay informed**: Short selling requires constant monitoring and analysis to stay informed about market conditions and potential risks. Staying up-to-date on market news and trends can help identify potential opportunities and risks, and help inform your investment decisions.

- **Monitor your positions**: Regularly monitoring your short positions is vital to ensure that they are performing as expected and to make any necessary adjustments. Being vigilant and attentive to market movements and changes in your investment thesis can enable you to stay ahead of potential risks.

- **Diversify your portfolio**: Diversification is key to spreading risk and mitigating the impact of any single investment. This is particularly important when short selling, as the potential for unlimited losses is inherent in the strategy. By diversifying your portfolio, you can protect yourself from any unforeseen risks that may arise.

Examples:

Enron Collapse (2001): A prime illustration of short selling's potency can be traced back to the downfall of Enron, an energy company that once ranked among America's corporate giants. Short sellers, led by investor Jim Chanos, identified inconsistencies in Enron's financial statements and surmised that the company's stock was significantly overvalued. By borrowing and selling Enron's shares and subsequently repurchasing them at a fraction of the initial selling price following the company's collapse, these astute investors reaped substantial profits.

Volkswagen Short Squeeze (2008): A cautionary tale for short sellers unfolded during the 2008 Volkswagen short squeeze. Porsche, in a covert move, acquired a controlling stake in Volkswagen, causing the latter's share price to soar. Short sellers, who had anticipated a decline in Volkswagen's stock value, were caught off guard and faced astronomical losses as they scrambled to repurchase shares at vastly inflated prices to cover their positions.

Bill Ackman's Herbalife Short (2012): The Herbalife saga demonstrates the potential pitfalls of short selling, even for seasoned investors. Hedge fund manager Bill Ackman famously shorted the nutrition company Herbalife, accusing it of being a pyramid scheme. Despite his confident claims, Herbalife's stock price did not collapse as anticipated, and Ackman eventually closed his short position in 2018, suffering a reported loss of around $1 billion.

Tesla Short Sellers (2020): Tesla's meteoric rise in stock price during 2020 provided a striking example of the perils of short selling amidst surging market enthusiasm. As the electric vehicle manufacturer's stock price skyrocketed, short sellers, who had bet against the company's success, experienced mounting losses. According to some estimates, Tesla short sellers lost over $38 billion in 2020 alone. This example underscores the potential risks associated with short selling, particularly when market sentiment and momentum diverge from the short seller's expectations.

These instances exemplify the intricate dynamics of short selling, highlighting both the triumphs and tribulations that may arise for investors who venture into this complex financial sphere.

Useful resources to analyze Short Selling data

ShortSqueeze.com: ShortSqueeze offers a wide array of data relating to short selling. It provides information about short interest, short squeeze rankings, and short interest ratios. It also has a screening tool to identify stocks with high short interest.

FINRA's Short Interest: The Financial Industry Regulatory Authority (FINRA) offers a database on short interest which is reported by all FINRA member firms twice a month. This data can be used to analyze the level of short interest in individual securities.

HighShortInterest.com: This website provides a list of stocks with high short interest in the market. It's a simple resource that can be used to quickly identify potential targets of short selling.

Yahoo Finance: While Yahoo Finance offers a broad range of financial data and news, it also provides data related to short selling. You can find information such as short percent of float and short percent of shares outstanding in the statistics section for each stock.

Summary

Within the sphere of investment, short selling unveils itself as a captivating and intriguing practice, enabling investors to garner monetary advantages from the reduction in a stock's value. This technique diverges from the customary tactic of amassing profits by buying at a low cost and selling at an elevated one; rather, it hinges upon anticipating a downturn in a security's worth. Short selling can serve as a potent instrument for investors, presenting opportunities to secure gains in adverse markets and establishing a safeguard against unfettered optimism. However, this intricate financial gambit encompasses inherent perils, such as the prospect of infinite losses, regulatory limitations, and market instability.

To carry out a short selling operation, an investor is required to borrow a security, dispose of it, reacquire it at a decreased price, and return it to the lender, retaining the differential as income. There are diverse short selling approaches, each with its unique array of hazards and returns. For example, naked short selling is considered unlawful in most legal frameworks, while covered short selling constitutes a more conventional method that adheres to legal mandates. Short selling on margin holds the power to intensify potential profits or losses, and short selling against the box can act as a tax-deferral mechanism. Simultaneously, short selling ETFs offers an avenue to exploit the decline of the foundational assets overseen by these funds.

To determine the most suitable short selling strategy, an investor must grasp their ambitions, the associated risks, and the character of the security being exchanged. Furthermore, they should assess market circumstances, opt for the fitting timing and modus operandi, implement short selling stratagems, and stay abreast of potential hazards and prospects. While short selling affords a distinct chance to attain profits in depreciating markets, investors must contemplate the risks and impediments in contrast to the potential rewards, and ascertain that they hold a thorough understanding of the complexities involved before embarking upon this convoluted financial domain.

Part V

Investment Tools and Techniques

Chapter 18

Fundamental Analysis

Fundamental analysis serves as the bedrock of astute investing, offering a systematic approach to assessing the intrinsic value of securities. By examining financial statements, economic indicators, and market factors, investors can make informed decisions to buy, sell, or hold specific stocks or other securities.

This chapter aims to provide a comprehensive exploration of fundamental analysis, focusing on its principles, methodologies, and practical applications.

In this chapter, we will delve into the three primary facets of fundamental analysis: quantitative, qualitative, and macroeconomic analysis. Each of these components plays a crucial role in providing a holistic understanding of a company's value and potential.

Quantitative analysis, involves a meticulous evaluation of a company's financial statements and valuation metrics, enabling investors to gain insights into the firm's financial health and performance.

Qualitative analysis, focuses on intangible factors such as management quality, corporate governance, and industry dynamics, shedding light on a company's competitive position and long-term prospects.

Macroeconomic analysis, examines the broader economic landscape, assessing the impact of economic indicators, fiscal policies, and global economic interdependence on security valuations.

Additionally, we will explore **consolidative and practical applications** that combine the knowledge gained from fundamental analysis with other essential concepts in investing. This section will cover the integration of fundamental analysis with technical analysis, the influence of behavioral finance on decision-making, the role of investor sentiment and market psychology, and the importance of managing cognitive biases and emotional traps. Additionally, we will discuss the principles of diversification and risk management strategies, which are integral to constructing a resilient and well-balanced investment portfolio.

I. Quantitative Analysis

1. Financial Statement Analysis

Financial statements provide essential insights into a company's financial health. By dissecting these documents, investors can gain a deep understanding of a firm's underlying value and potential.

A. Components of financial statements

i. Balance sheet: A snapshot of a company's assets, liabilities, and shareholders' equity at a specific point in time, highlighting the firm's financial position.

Example: A strong balance sheet might show a growing amount of cash and assets, alongside manageable liabilities, suggesting the company is in a stable financial position.

Item	Company A	Company B
Assets		
Current Assets	500,000	750,000
Fixed Assets	1,000,000	1,250,000
Intangible Assets	200,000	300,000
Total Assets	1,700,000	2,300,000
Liabilities		
Current Liabilities	200,000	500,000
Long-term Liabilities	800,000	1,000,000
Total Liabilities	1,000,000	1,500,000
Shareholders' Equity		
Common Stock	200,000	300,000
Retained Earnings	500,000	500,000
Total Shareholders' Equity	700,000	800,000
Total Liabilities and Shareholders' Equity	1,700,000	2,300,000

Figure 18.1: Balance Sheet

In **Figure 18.1**, upon examining the balance sheets of both Company A and Company B, it is evident that Company B possesses a larger asset base. However, it is crucial to delve deeper into the composition of these assets. Company A's current assets are proportionally higher than Company B's, suggesting better short-term liquidity. In terms of liabilities, Company B has higher overall liabilities, which could indicate higher financial risk.

The debt-to-equity ratio (not provided in the table) can provide further insight into the companies' solvency. Comparing shareholders' equity reveals that Company A retains a larger portion of its earnings, which may signal greater financial stability and potential for future growth.

ii. Income statement: A record of a company's revenue, expenses, and profit over a given period, offering insights into the company's financial performance and profitability.

Example: A robust income statement may display consistent revenue growth and expanding profit margins, indicating the company is effectively managing costs and generating profits.

Item	Company A	Company B
Revenue	1,500,000	2,000,000
Cost of Goods Sold (COGS)	(900,000)	(1,200,000)
Gross Profit	600,000	800,000
Operating Expenses	(300,000)	(400,000)
Operating Income	300,000	400,000
Interest Expense	(50,000)	(100,000)
Income Tax Expense	(60,000)	(80,000)
Net Income	190,000	220,000

Figure 18.2: Income Statement

The income statements reveal that Company B generates more revenue than Company A. However, it is vital to evaluate the firms' profitability margins, such as the gross profit margin and operating margin. Although Company B has higher gross profit, Company A appears to have better cost control, as evidenced by its higher gross profit margin. Additionally, Company A's operating margin surpasses Company B's, indicating superior operational efficiency. In terms of net income, both companies display healthy earnings, but a closer examination of their respective net profit margins could provide further clarity on their overall profitability.

iii. Cash flow statement: A summary of the inflows and outflows of cash from operating, investing, and financing activities, shedding light on a company's liquidity and solvency.

Example: A healthy cash flow statement might show positive cash flow from operations, indicating the company's core business is generating sufficient cash to support its activities.

By analyzing the cash flow statement, we can observe how the cash flows from operating, investing, and financing activities contribute to the overall cash position of both companies.

In **Figure 18.3**, Company A has a positive net cash flow of 80,000 (230,000 - 200,000 + 50,000), while Company B has a net cash flow of 100,000 (310,000 - 300,000 + 90,000). Comparing the two companies, we can see that Company B generates higher cash flow from its operating activities, while Company A has a more conservative investment approach, resulting in lower capital expenditures and investments.

Item	Company A	Company B
Operating Activities		
Net Income	190,000	220,000
Depreciation	50,000	70,000
Changes in Working Capital	(10,000)	20,000
Net Cash from Operating Activities	230,000	310,000
Investing Activities		
Capital Expenditures	(150,000)	(200,000)
Investments	(50,000)	(100,000)
Net Cash from Investing Activities	(200,000)	(300,000)
Financing Activities		
Issuance of Stock	100,000	150,000
Dividends Paid	(50,000)	(60,000)
Net Cash from Financing Activities	50,000	90,000

Figure 18.3: Cash Flow Statement

iv. Statement of shareholders' equity: A report that demonstrates the changes in a company's equity over a period, accounting for factors such as share issuances, buybacks, and changes in retained earnings.

Example: A positive statement of shareholders' equity may exhibit an increasing retained earnings balance, reflecting the company's ability to reinvest profits for growth.

Figure 18.4 presents the statement of shareholders' equity for Example Company A and Example Company B. We can observe the changes in shareholders' equity over the period, considering the issuance of stock, net income, and dividends paid.

Both companies, shareholders' equity has increased over the period. Company A's shareholders' equity increased by 240,000 (100,000 + 190,000 - 50,000), while Company B's increased by 310,000 (150,000 + 220,000 - 60,000).

Item	Company A	Company B
Beginning Shareholders' Equity		
Common Stock	300,000	400,000
Retained Earnings	200,000	250,000
Total Beginning Shareholders' Equity	500,000	650,000
Changes in Shareholders' Equity		
Issuance of Stock	100,000	150,000
Net Income	190,000	220,000
Dividends Paid	(50,000)	(60,000)
Total Changes in Shareholders' Equity	240,000	310,000
Ending Shareholders' Equity		
Common Stock	400,000	550,000
Retained Earnings	340,000	410,000
Total Ending Shareholders' Equity	740,000	960,000

Figure 18.4: Statement of shareholders' equity

By examining the statement of shareholders' equity, investors can gain insights into the company's financial position and evaluate how effectively the company is using its equity to generate returns.

B. Earnings quality assessment

A meticulous examination of the reliability and sustainability of a company's earnings, the earnings quality assessment delves beyond superficial figures to uncover the true essence of a firm's financial performance. This process entails scrutinizing factors such as revenue recognition policies, consistency in earnings growth, and the sustainability of profit margins, enabling investors to gauge the underlying strength of a company's financial position.

Example: Consider a popular e-commerce company that has consistently reported increasing earnings over the past five years. Upon closer investigation, an investor using a well-known financial analysis website, such as Seeking Alpha, discovers that a substantial portion of the growth stems from one-time gains, such as asset sales or tax benefits, and aggressive revenue recognition policies, rather than from core business operations.

For instance, the investor may find the information on the website as elucidated in **Figure 18.5**.

In this case, the company's earnings quality may be deemed lower, suggesting that its financial performance may not be as reliable and sustainable as initially perceived, which could impact the investor's decision-making process.

Year	Reported Earnings	Core Earnings	One-time Gains
1	$100 million	$90 million	$10 million
2	$120 million	$100 million	$20 million
3	$150 million	$110 million	$40 million

Figure 18.5: Earnings quality assessment

C. Financial modeling techniques

Sophisticated tools that empower investors to project a company's future financial performance, financial modeling techniques offer valuable insights for informed decision-making. Financial modeling encompasses the construction of a comprehensive representation of a company's financials, incorporating assumptions about various factors such as future revenue growth, cost structures, and industry trends. This model serves as a versatile instrument for conducting sensitivity analyses, evaluating investment opportunities, and assessing the impact of potential strategic decisions.

Example: An investor seeks to value a promising renewable energy company expected to experience rapid growth over the next five years. Utilizing a renowned financial analysis website, such as Yahoo Finance, the investor constructs a financial model that forecasts the company's revenue, expenses, and profits for this period, factoring in elements such as market share, pricing trends, and operating leverage.

The investor may create a table with assumptions, as illustrated in **Figure 18.6**.

By fine-tuning these assumptions, the investor can assess the company's sensitivity to diverse scenarios, enabling them to ascertain if the stock is undervalued or overvalued based on various growth expectations. This information can significantly influence the investor's decision to buy, hold, or sell the stock, ultimately refining their investment strategy.

	Year 1	Year 2	Year 3
Revenue Growth	20%	25%	30%
Market Share	10%	12%	15%
Operating Leverage	1.5	1.4	1.3
Projected Revenue	$50 million	$62.5 million	$81.25 million
Projected Expenses	$40 million	$47 million	$58 million
Projected Profits	$10 million	$15.5 million	$23.25 million

Figure 18.6: Financial modeling

2. Financial Ratios and Valuation Techniques

Financial ratios and valuation techniques are essential tools for investors to assess a company's financial health and determine the fair value of its securities, guiding them toward informed choices.

A. Financial Ratios

i. **Liquidity Ratios**: Assess a company's ability to meet short-term obligations, revealing the firm's financial flexibility.

Formula: Current Ratio = Current Assets / Current Liabilities

Example: To illustrate liquidity analysis, consider Company A with $1 million in current assets and $500,000 in current liabilities. The Current Ratio (Current Assets / Current Liabilities) would be 2 (1,000,000 / 500,000), suggesting a strong liquidity position. This means the company can comfortably meet its short-term obligations without financial strain, which is an attractive characteristic for potential investors.

ii. **Solvency Ratios**: Evaluate a company's long-term financial stability, illustrating the firm's capacity to meet its long-term debt commitments.

Formula: Debt-to-Equity Ratio = Total Debt / Total Shareholders' Equity

Example: Let's examine Company B with $2 million in total debt and $4 million in total shareholders' equity. The Debt-to-Equity Ratio (Total Debt / Total Shareholders' Equity) would be 0.5 (2,000,000 / 4,000,000), indicating a manageable debt burden. A low ratio implies that the company relies more on equity financing than debt, reducing the risk of default and making it more attractive to investors.

iii. **Profitability Ratios**: Measure a company's ability to generate profits, indicating the efficiency and effectiveness of its operations.

Formula: Net Profit Margin = Net Income / Revenue

Example: Consider Company C with net income of $150,000 and revenue of $1 million. The Net Profit Margin (Net Income / Revenue) would be 15% (150,000 / 1,000,000), reflecting strong profitability. This indicates that the company retains $0.15 of profit for every $1 of revenue generated, making it potentially appealing to investors looking for profitable investments.

iv. **Efficiency Ratios**: Analyze how well a company utilizes its assets and resources, reflecting the firm's operational prowess.

Formula: Asset Turnover Ratio = Revenue / Average Total Assets

Example: Let's examine Company D with $5 million in revenue and $2.5 million in average total assets. The Asset Turnover Ratio (Revenue / Average Total Assets) would be 2 (5,000,000 / 2,500,000), suggesting efficient asset utilization. This means the company generates $2 in revenue for every $1 of assets, indicating effective use of resources and strong operational prowess.

B. Valuation Techniques

i. **Price-to-Earnings (P/E) Ratio**: A popular benchmark that compares a company's stock price to its earnings per share, providing a standardized metric for valuation.

Formula: P/E Ratio = Stock Price / Earnings per Share

Example: Consider a company with a stock price of $50 and earnings per share of $5. The P/E Ratio (Stock Price / Earnings per Share) would be 10 (50 / 5), suggesting that investors are willing to pay $10 for every $1 of earnings. Comparing this ratio to industry peers can help determine if the stock is overvalued or undervalued, guiding investment decisions.

ii. **Price-to-Sales (P/S) Ratio**: A valuation ratio that compares a company's stock price to its revenue per share, providing a useful metric for assessing the company's valuation relative to its sales performance.

Formula: P/S Ratio = Stock Price / Revenue per Share

Example: For a company in a rapidly growing industry with a stock price of $100 and revenue per share of $50, the P/S Ratio (Stock Price / Revenue per Share) would be 2 (100 / 50). Comparing this ratio to other companies within the same industry can help identify potential investment opportunities, as a lower ratio may indicate an undervalued stock.

iii. **Price-to-Book (P/B) Ratio**: A comparison of a company's market value to its book value, offering insights into how the market perceives the company's net worth.

Formula: P/B Ratio = Stock Price / Book Value per Share

Example: Suppose a company's stock is trading at $60, and its book value per share is $40. The P/B Ratio (Stock Price / Book Value per Share) would be 1.5 (60 / 40). A ratio higher than 1 might indicate that the market perceives the company to have growth potential or a strong competitive advantage, warranting further analysis to determine if the stock is an attractive investment.

iv. **Enterprise Value-to-EBITDA (EV/EBITDA) Ratio**: A comprehensive measure that considers a company's entire capital structure, comparing its enterprise value to earnings before interest, taxes, depreciation, and amortization.

Formula: EV/EBITDA Ratio = Enterprise Value / EBITDA

Example: Consider a company with an enterprise value of $80 million and EBITDA of $10 million. The EV/EBITDA Ratio (Enterprise Value / EBITDA) would be 8 (80,000,000 / 10,000,000). A lower ratio, compared to industry peers, might signal that the stock is undervalued, presenting a potential investment opportunity for investors who are seeking exposure to companies with strong cash flow generation and manageable debt levels.

v. **Dividend Discount Model (DDM) and Discounted Cash Flow Model (DCF)**: Both are sophisticated financial valuation methodologies that adeptly assess the intrinsic worth of a stock. By calculating the present value of anticipated future cash flows, these models account for the time value of money and empower investors to make well-informed investment decisions.

The **DDM** is particularly valuable for income-focused investors, as it emphasizes the estimation of a stock's intrinsic value based on the present value of prospective future dividend payments.

Formula: DDM = Dividend per Share / (Discount Rate - Dividend Growth Rate). Here, the dividend per share signifies the company's projected future dividends, the discount rate embodies the required rate of return, and the dividend growth rate denotes the expected rate of dividend growth.

Conversely, the **DCF** Model ascertains the present value of a company's predicted future cash flows, such as earnings or profits, by factoring in the time value of money.

Formula: DCF = $\sum$ (Cash Flow / (1 + Discount Rate) ^Period), wherein the cash flow represents the company's estimated future earnings, the discount rate accommodates the required rate of return, and the period corresponds to when the cash flow is anticipated to be received.

Both the DDM and DCF Model meticulously adjust future cash flows to their present value, facilitating a seamless comparison to a company's existing market value. By employing these intricate valuation techniques, investors can glean insights into a stock's potential worth.

Example to illustrate the DDM: Consider a stock with an annual dividend per share of $2, a discount rate of 8%, and a dividend growth rate of 2%. The DDM (Dividend per Share / (Discount Rate - Dividend Growth Rate)) would be $2 / (0.08 - 0.02) = $33.33. By comparing the intrinsic value calculated using the DDM to the stock's current market price, an investor can determine if the stock is overvalued or undervalued, allowing them to evaluate its income potential relative to its market price.

Example to illustrate the DCF: Let's assume an investor estimates a company's future cash flows as follows: $1 million for Year 1, $1.2 million for Year 2, $1.4 million for Year 3, and $1.6 million for Year 4. The investor uses a discount rate of 10%. The DCF formula is applied to each year's cash flow, summing the results to obtain the present value:

Year 1: $1,000,000 / (1 + 0.1) ^1 = $909,091
Year 2: $1,200,000 / (1 + 0.1) ^2 = $990,826
Year 3: $1,400,000 / (1 + 0.1) ^3 = $1,026,157
Year 4: $1,600,000 / (1 + 0.1) ^4 = $1,037,619
Total Present Value: $3,963,693

Comparing the present value of projected cash flows to the company's market capitalization helps investors determine if a stock is trading above or below its intrinsic value.

To better comprehend the terminologies used in the DDM and DCF, let's break down each component:

1. **Intrinsic Value**: The intrinsic value of a stock refers to its true, inherent worth, as opposed to its market price, which is influenced by external factors like market sentiment and trading volumes. Estimating the intrinsic value helps investors determine if a stock is overvalued or undervalued.
2. **Dividend**: A dividend is a payment made by a corporation to its shareholders, typically in the

form of cash or additional shares, as a distribution of profits.

3. **Dividend per Share**: Dividend per Share (DPS) is the amount of dividend paid to each shareholder for each share they own. It is calculated by dividing the total dividend payment by the number of outstanding shares.

4. **Present Value**: The present value of a future cash flow, such as a dividend payment, represents its current worth, taking into account the time value of money.

5. **Time Value**: The time value of money suggests that a dollar received today is worth more than a dollar received in the future because the dollar received today can be invested and grow in value over time.

6. **Discount Rate**: The discount rate is the rate of return required by an investor to invest in a stock. It reflects the investor's opportunity cost, which is the return they could have earned from an alternative investment with a similar risk profile. The discount rate is used to discount future cash flows, such as dividends, to their present value.

7. **Dividend Growth Rate**: The dividend growth rate is the annual percentage increase in a company's dividend per share. A positive dividend growth rate indicates that a company is consistently increasing its dividend payments, which is generally seen as a sign of financial strength and stability.

Summary

Quantitative analysis is an indispensable and sophisticated approach utilized by astute investors and financial analysts to meticulously assess investment prospects through the lens of mathematical and statistical methodologies. By systematically dissecting numerical data, this powerful technique facilitates an objective appraisal of a company's financial well-being, prevailing market trends, and underlying risk factors.

Quantitative analysis bolsters informed decision-making by delivering valuable insights into performance indicators, valuation ratios, and potential growth catalysts, ultimately refining the precision and effectiveness of investment strategies. In essence, quantitative analysis serves as a vital cornerstone for data-driven investment decisions, fostering a comprehensive understanding of the investment landscape and engendering more accurate prognostications.

II. Qualitative Analysis

Qualitative analysis is an indispensable component of fundamental analysis that focuses on non-quantifiable factors affecting a company's performance and value. It provides investors with a broader perspective on a company's prospects by examining its internal dynamics, competitive environment, and industry trends.

1. Company Analysis

A. Business model assessment:

i. Customer value proposition: The unique combination of products, services, and experiences a company offers to its customers to meet their needs and create value. For example, Apple's value proposition is built around innovation, user-friendly design, and a seamless ecosystem.

ii. Profit formula: The way a company generates revenue and profit through its pricing strategy, cost structure, and sales volume. For example, Amazon's profit formula relies on high sales volumes, efficient logistics, and a diverse range of products and services.

iii. Key resources and processes: The essential assets and operational activities that enable a company to deliver its value proposition and maintain a competitive advantage. For instance, Tesla's key resources include its electric vehicle technology, battery production, and charging infrastructure.

B. Management quality evaluation: An assessment of the effectiveness, experience, and integrity of a company's leadership team. This may include evaluating their track record of success, strategic vision, and ability to navigate challenges. For example, Warren Buffett's leadership at Berkshire Hathaway exemplifies strong management quality.

C. Corporate governance practices: The system of rules, practices, and processes by which a company is directed and controlled. Strong corporate governance practices include a diverse and independent board of directors, transparent reporting, and well-defined decision-making processes.

D. Environmental, social, and governance (ESG) factors: Criteria that measure a company's ethical, sustainable, and responsible practices. Investors increasingly consider ESG factors to gauge a company's long-term viability and potential risks. For instance, Patagonia's commitment to environmental sustainability and fair labor practices is a strong ESG performance indicator.

2. Industry and Competitive Analysis

A. Industry life cycle analysis: The examination of an industry's maturity stage, from inception to growth, maturity, and decline. Understanding an industry's life cycle stage helps investors identify opportunities and risks associated with market dynamics. For example, the smartphone industry is currently in the maturity stage, with slower growth and increased competition.

B. Porter's Five Forces framework: A widely-used tool to assess the competitive forces within an industry: rivalry among existing competitors, threats of new entrants, bargaining power of suppliers, bargaining power of buyers, and threats of substitute products or services. For example, applying Porter's Five Forces to the airline industry reveals high competition, low barriers to entry, and significant bargaining power for both suppliers and customers.

C. Identifying industry trends and disruptions: The process of recognizing emerging patterns and transformative changes in an industry that may create new opportunities or challenges. For example, the rise of electric vehicles has disrupted the traditional automotive industry, posing a threat to incumbent manufacturers and creating opportunities for new entrants like Tesla.

D. Innovation and technological advancements: The role of ground-breaking technologies and novel solutions in shaping industries and driving competitive advantages. For instance, the development of artificial intelligence and machine learning has revolutionized various industries, including healthcare, finance, and manufacturing.

Summary

Qualitative analysis is a crucial aspect of evaluating potential investments, as it delves into the non-numerical factors that influence a company's performance and prospects. By examining aspects such as management quality, competitive advantage, industry dynamics, and the regulatory environment, investors can gain a deeper understanding of a company's potential for success.

Incorporating qualitative analysis into the decision-making process enables investors to identify promising opportunities and mitigate risks, complementing quantitative methods to form a comprehensive assessment of an investment's overall attractiveness.

III. Macroeconomic Analysis

Macroeconomic analysis is a vital aspect of fundamental analysis that examines the broader economic environment and its influence on security valuation. It helps investors understand the interplay between economic indicators, monetary and fiscal policy, and global economic trends, allowing them to make more informed investment decisions.

1. Economic indicators and their impact on security valuation

A. Gross Domestic Product (GDP): The total value of all goods and services produced in an economy over a specific period, representing a country's overall economic health. A growing GDP can signal a healthy economy and may lead to higher corporate earnings and stock prices.

B. Inflation: The rate at which the general level of prices for goods and services is rising, leading to a decrease in purchasing power. High inflation erodes the real value of investments and can cause central banks to increase interest rates. For instance, if inflation rises above the Federal Reserve's target, it may result in higher interest rates, negatively impacting bond prices and raising borrowing costs for companies.

C. Interest rates: The cost of borrowing money, set by central banks as a tool to control inflation and stimulate economic growth. Changes in interest rates can significantly impact security valuations, as higher interest rates increase borrowing costs, potentially lowering corporate earnings and stock prices. For example, an unexpected interest rate hike by the Federal Reserve can lead to a decline in the stock market.

D. Unemployment rate: The percentage of the labor force that is without a job but actively seeking employment. A high unemployment rate can indicate a weak economy, while a low rate may signal a strong economy with potential inflationary pressures. For instance, a rising unemployment rate during a recession may lead to lower consumer spending, negatively impacting corporate earnings and stock prices.

E. Consumer sentiment: A measure of consumer confidence in the economy, based on their willingness to spend and overall economic outlook. High consumer sentiment can lead to increased spending and corporate earnings, positively impacting stock prices. For example, a strong consumer sentiment reading may suggest a robust economy, potentially benefiting consumer-focused companies and their stock prices.

2. The role of central banks and fiscal policy

Central banks, exemplified by the Federal Reserve in the US, serve as vital stewards of a nation's monetary policy, exercising authority over interest rates, money supply, and financial institution regulation. Their decisions wield considerable influence on security valuations, as alterations in interest rates or monetary policy invariably affect borrowing costs, investment yields, and the general market climate.

Concurrently, fiscal policy, shaped by governmental measures, encompasses the strategic manipulation of tax rates and public expenditure to foster economic expansion and stability. This policy exerts a tangible impact on corporate profitability and security valuations through fluctuations in taxation, infrastructural investments, and diverse government-driven initiatives. In essence, the interplay between central banks and fiscal policy forms the backbone of a nation's financial framework, steering its economic trajectory and shaping the valuation landscape for securities.

3. Global economic interdependence and currency fluctuations

In the intricately interwoven fabric of the modern global economy, occurrences in one nation can create ripple effects across the globe, directly influencing security valuations. Investors must account for a multitude of worldwide economic factors, such as trade policies, geopolitical developments, and regional growth dynamics when scrutinizing securities.

Simultaneously, currency fluctuations wield substantial sway over security valuations, particularly for multinational corporations operating in multiple nations. Exchange rate shifts can alter a company's revenue, expenses, and profits when recalculated into its domestic currency. For instance, a depreciating US dollar could amplify the earnings of US-based firms with considerable international operations, as their overseas profits appreciate in value upon conversion to dollars.

Summary

Macroeconomic analysis represents a thorough exploration of grand-scale economic elements that influence financial markets and steer investment decision-making. By diligently examining pivotal indicators such as GDP growth, inflation, interest rates, fiscal and monetary policies, alongside global economic trends and currency fluctuations, investors acquire essential insights into the overarching economic landscape.

This comprehension of macroeconomic intricacies empowers investors to skillfully traverse the complexities of financial markets, pinpoint lucrative opportunities, mitigate inherent risks, and ultimately, make astute decisions in a perpetually evolving and interconnected economic milieu. Possessing a solid foundation in macroeconomic analysis, investors are better prepared to foresee and adjust to the potential ramifications of economic shifts on security valuations.

IV. Consolidative and Practical Application

Fundamental analysis, while a potent tool, can be enhanced when integrated with other investment approaches and strategies. This section delves into how investors can combine various techniques to make well-rounded decisions and manage risk in their portfolios effectively.

1. Integrating fundamental analysis with technical analysis

Fundamental analysis focuses on assessing a company's financial health and intrinsic value, while technical analysis examines historical price patterns and trends to predict future price movements. By fusing these two approaches, investors can pinpoint undervalued or overvalued stocks and take market momentum and timing into account. For instance, an investor may discover a fundamentally robust company trading at a discount to its intrinsic value and utilize technical analysis to identify the optimal entry point based on support and resistance levels.

2. Behavioral Finance: Influencing Decision-Making

Behavioral finance investigates the impact of psychological factors and biases on investors' decision-making processes. By recognizing and understanding these biases, investors can make more rational decisions and sidestep common pitfalls. For example, being aware of confirmation bias, which leads individuals to seek out information confirming their pre-existing beliefs, can prompt investors to actively challenge their assumptions and consider alternative viewpoints.

3. Investor Sentiment and Market Psychology

Investor sentiment and market psychology can significantly affect security prices, often causing temporary deviations from their intrinsic value. Analyzing market sentiment and comprehending the psychological factors driving investor behavior can help investors identify potential market inefficiencies and capitalize on them. For instance, during periods of extreme pessimism or optimism, investors may uncover opportunities to purchase undervalued stocks or sell overvalued ones.

4. Managing Cognitive Biases and Emotional Traps

Cognitive biases and emotional traps can impede an investor's ability to make objective, rational decisions. By identifying these biases and employing strategies to counteract them, investors can enhance their decision-making process. For example, establishing a systematic investment approach and maintaining a long-term perspective can assist investors in avoiding the pitfalls of short-term thinking and emotional decision-making.

5. Diversification and Risk Management Strategies

Diversification is a vital risk management strategy that involves spreading investments across various asset classes, industries, and regions to mitigate portfolio risk. By blending securities with differing risk and return characteristics, investors can achieve a more balanced portfolio that is less vulnerable to market fluctuations. For instance, an investor may diversify their portfolio by investing in a mix of stocks, bonds, and real estate across different sectors and countries, reducing the impact of a downturn in any single market or industry.

Summary

Fundamental analysis serves as a vital cornerstone for appraising the intrinsic value of securities, empowering investors to make judicious decisions when purchasing, liquidating, or retaining various financial instruments. By meticulously examining financial statements, qualitative aspects, and macroeconomic indicators, investors unveil a wealth of insights into a company's fiscal well-being, competitive positioning, and the overarching economic climate, ultimately unearthing hidden investment opportunities and discerning the authentic potential of securities.

When synergistically integrated with other investment approaches, such as technical analysis, behavioral finance, and risk management strategies, fundamental analysis acquires an even more potent efficacy. By embracing a comprehensive and holistic approach to decision-making, investors can proficiently traverse the intricate landscape of financial markets, pinpoint undervalued or overvalued assets, skillfully manage risks, and ultimately achieve exceptional investment results.

Chapter 19

Technical Analysis

In the enormous and vibrant world of investing, technical analysis stands as a powerful conductor, orchestrating a symphony of market trends, patterns, and indicators that guide traders on their path to financial success.

Unlike its counterpart, fundamental analysis, technical analysis focuses on the "what" rather than the "why" of price movements. By observing the market's past behavior, technical analysts aim to predict its future trajectory.

It is substantiated in the belief that market participants exhibit collective behaviors that can be observed, interpreted, and leveraged to make profitable trading decisions. The foundation of technical analysis lies in three key principles:

1. **Market action discounts everything**: All known and relevant information is already reflected in an asset's price, debatably rendering fundamental and economic analysis unnecessary for identifying profitable trades.

2. **Prices move in trends**: The movement of asset prices is not random but follows trends that persist over time, whether bullish, bearish, or sideways.

3. **History tends to repeat itself**: Market participants' psychological behaviors create recurring patterns in price movements that can be recognized and exploited to anticipate future price action.

The Core of Technical Analysis: Price and Volume

Technical analysis relies on the fundamental relationship between price and volume to interpret the market's behavior and forecast future price movements. These two components represent the collective decisions and emotions of market participants, providing valuable insights into the market's underlying dynamics.

Price: The Market's Primary Signal

Price is the primary means of communication for the market, reflecting the collective sentiment of all participants. As investors react to new information and events, their actions create price fluctuations, which in turn reveal essential information about the market's direction and strength.

Technical indicators such as moving averages and oscillators also derive from price data, providing additional context for the market's behavior and potential shifts in sentiment.

Volume: The Market's Activity Indicator

Volume, which measures the trading activity within a given period, serves as a crucial indicator of market participation and interest. In technical analysis, volume plays an essential role in confirming price movements and providing insight into the strength or weakness of a trend.

When price and volume move together, it suggests a credible and strong trend.

Example: An upward price movement accompanied by increasing volume indicates solid buying pressure and a robust bullish trend. On the other hand, a downward price movement with rising volume points to strong selling pressure and a bearish trend.

However, when price and volume diverge, it may hint at potential trend reversals or a loss of momentum. For instance, if an asset's price reaches new highs but the trading volume does not follow, this discrepancy may signal a lack of conviction among buyers, increasing the likelihood of a trend reversal.

Table 19.1 illustrates how the amalgamation of price movement and volume can signal different market trends and their potential interpretations.

Support, Resistance, and Trend is explained in the subsequent section.

Price Movement	Volume	Trend	Interpretation
Increase	High	Bullish	Strong buying demand, potential trend reversal, break from previous resistance
Decrease	High	Bearish	Strong selling pressure, potential trend reversal, break from previous support
Increase	Low	Neutral	Weak buying, potential trend continuation, no break from previous resistance
Decrease	Low	Neutral	Weak selling, potential trend continuation, no break from previous support
Stagnant	High	Neutral	High volatility, indecision in market, caution required
Stagnant	Low	Neutral	Lack of participation in market, caution required, low liquidity

Table 19.1: Price Movement and Volume

The Art of Chart Analysis

To master the art of chart analysis, one must learn to identify key elements such as trends, support and resistance levels, chart patterns, and technical indicators. The selection of an appropriate time frame is crucial, as it reflects the analyst's unique perspective and investment horizon. Short-term traders may opt for hourly or daily charts, while long-term investors might prefer weekly or monthly charts to capture broader trends. By understanding these components, investors can create a cohesive narrative of the market's performance and predict its future movements.

The Building Blocks: Support, Resistance, and Trend Lines

The foundations of technical analysis rest on three vital concepts: support, resistance, and trend lines.

Figure 19.1: Support, Resistance and Trend Lines

Support: A price level where buying pressure consistently emerges, preventing the asset's price from falling further.

- **Significance**: Identifies potential entry points for long positions, helps in setting stop-loss orders, and serves as a basis for determining trend reversals.

Resistance: A price level where selling pressure consistently materializes, halting the asset's upward price movement.

- **Significance**: Identifies potential entry points for short positions, helps in setting profit targets, and serves as a basis for determining trend reversals.

Trend Lines: Lines connecting consecutive price points, revealing the direction and strength of the underlying trend, whether it's an upward surge, a downward spiral, or a tranquil period of consolidation.

- **Significance**: Assists in identifying trend direction, potential trend reversals, and potential breakout points.

- **Types**: Upward trend line (bullish), downward trend line (bearish), or consolidation (neutral).

- **Uptrends**: An uptrend is characterized by a series of higher highs and higher lows, reflecting a bullish market sentiment. Traders and investors should consider long positions in such scenarios and employ appropriate risk management strategies to protect profits and limit losses. Identifying a strong uptrend may also present opportunities to enter the market on minor retracements or consolidations within the prevailing trend.

- **Downtrends**: Downtrends are marked by a sequence of lower lows and lower highs, indicating bearish market conditions. In these circumstances, traders might opt for short-selling or implementing other bearish strategies to capitalize on the market's downward trajectory. Recognizing a robust downtrend allows traders to seek entry points during minor rallies or consolidations within the trend, while adhering to risk management principles.

- **Consolidation Phases**: A consolidation phase occurs when an asset's price moves sideways within a narrow range, reflecting market indecision and a balance between buying and selling pressure. Traders should exercise caution during these periods, as consolidation can precede a breakout or breakdown, leading to a new trend or a continuation of the existing trend. Patience and a keen eye for potential breakouts or breakdowns, accompanied by increased volume, can be advantageous for traders navigating consolidation phases.

Unraveling Market Trends and Dynamics

Table 19.2 Illustrates the Synthesis of Price Movement, and Market Trends Trading Interpretations:

- Probes the intricate relationship between price fluctuations and prevailing market trends, encompassing uptrends, downtrends, and consolidation phases.

- Stresses the cruciality of discerning breakouts above resistance or breakdowns below support, as well as the influence of consolidating markets.

- Provides actionable insights for traders based on the analysis of chart patterns and price movements.

Price Movement	Trend	Chart Analysis	Interpretation
Break above resistance	Uptrend	Bullish	**Buy signal**, potential trend reversal, prevailing buying demand
Break below support	Downtrend	Bearish	**Sell signal**, potential trend reversal, prevailing selling pressure
Higher highs and higher lows	Uptrend	Bullish	**Bullish** sign, robust buying demand, prospects for a continuing upward trend
Lower lows and lower highs	Downtrend	Bearish	**Bearish** sign, pronounced selling pressure, prospects for a trend reversal
Sideways	Consolidation	Neutral	**Hold**, market indecision, caution advised, potential for range-bound trading

Table 19.2: Price Movement and Market Trend, Trading Interpretations

Figures 19.2 and 19.3, highlights the importance of recognizing **higher highs and higher lows as bullish signals,** while **lower lows and lower highs signify bearish conditions**.

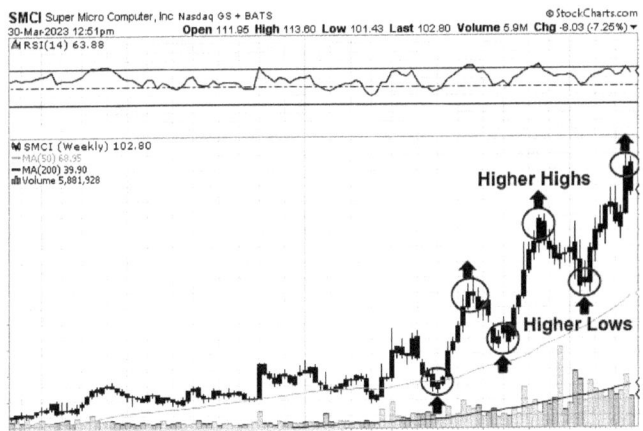

Figure 19.2: Higher Highs and Higher Lows (Bullish)

Figure 19.3: Lower Highs and Lower Lows (Bearish)

Technical Indicators

Figure 19.4 depicts Tesla's daily chart, while **Figure 19.5** outlines the chart attributes employed for analysis.

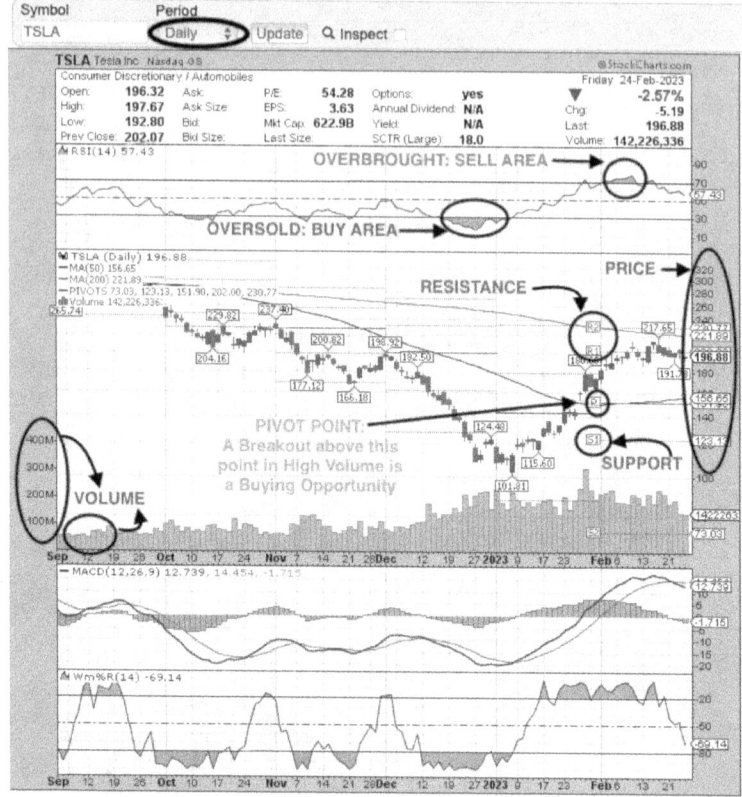

Figure 19.4: Tesla Daily Chart.
Source: StockCharts.com

- **Always compare both Daily and Weekly Charts to analyze proficiently.**

Figure 19.4 captures a multifaceted view of Tesla's daily chart, showcasing a blend of leading and lagging indicators. The chart displays the price and volume data, interwoven with support and resistance levels, offering subtle insights into potential buying opportunities upon high-volume breakouts above pivot points.

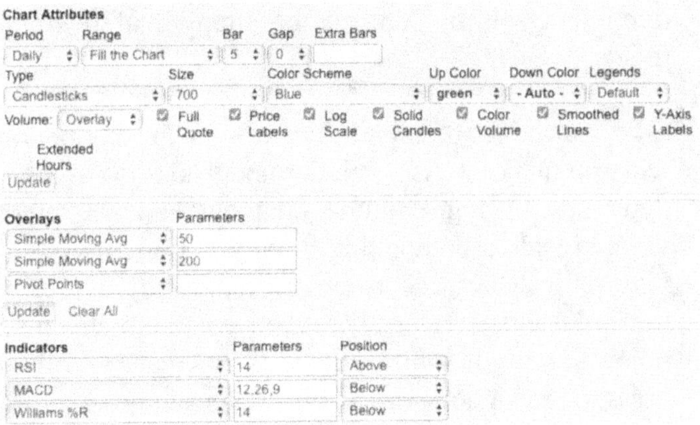

Figure 19.5: Chart Attributes used for Figure: 19.4

Technical indicators harmonize chart analysis, enriching insights into market dynamics through mathematical calculations based on price and volume data. They fall into two categories: leading and lagging.

Leading indicators, like the Relative Strength Index (RSI) and Moving Average Convergence Divergence (MACD), strive to predict future price movements. In contrast, lagging indicators, such as moving averages and Bollinger Bands, confirm existing trends and patterns.

Pivot points serve as nuanced technical indicators, adept at pinpointing potential support and resistance thresholds. Deriving their values from previous period's high, low, and closing prices, they operate in concert with other technical indicators to corroborate shifts in market trends. They are often used in conjunction with other technical indicators, such as moving averages, RSI, and MACD, to validate trend reversals or confirm the strength of ongoing trends.

Furthermore, monitoring volume in conjunction with pivot points is vital for understanding market dynamics. A high-volume breakout above a pivot point signals a compelling buying opportunity, as it may indicate a trend reversal or the start of a new upward trend. Conversely, a high-volume breakdown below a pivot point suggests increased selling pressure and a potential bearish reversal.

Moving averages serve as a vital analytical tool, computing the average price of an asset over a designated time frame and illustrating it on the chart. By smoothing out price fluctuations, moving averages enable investors to discern underlying trends more effectively. They function as reliable trend indicators, offering valuable insights into the asset's momentum and potential shifts in direction.

Two widely used moving averages in investing, as shown in Figure 5.2.4, are the 50-day (MA 50) and 200-day (MA 200) lines. The 50-day moving average captures short-term trends, while the 200-day moving average focuses on long-term movements. When a stock's price crosses above the 50-day or 200-day line, it may signal the commencement of a bullish trend. Conversely, when the price falls below these lines, a bearish trend may be underway. Additionally, the intersection of the 50-day and 200-day moving averages can signify a "golden cross" (bullish) or "death cross" (bearish), indicating a potential trend reversal.

Relative Strength Index (RSI), a leading indicator, is plotted with overbought and oversold regions, which signal potential reversals in price trends. It is calculated by comparing the magnitude of recent price gains to the magnitude of recent price losses and is plotted on a scale of 0 to 100. If the RSI is above 70, it may be considered overbought, and if it is below 30, it may be considered oversold.

Moving Average Convergence Divergence (MACD) is another leading indicator, highlighting shifts in momentum as the MACD line crosses the signal line (red line). It is computed by subtracting the value of a long-term moving average (typically a 26-day exponential moving average) from a short-term moving average (usually a 12-day exponential moving average). A signal line, which is a 9-day exponential moving average of the MACD itself, is then plotted alongside the MACD line.

The MACD offers valuable insights into potential buy and sell signals by analyzing the interactions between the MACD line and the signal line. When the MACD line crosses above the signal line, it indicates a potential buying opportunity, suggesting that the short-term momentum is increasing relative to the long-term momentum. Conversely, when the MACD line crosses below the signal line, it signals a potential selling opportunity, implying that the short-term momentum is decreasing compared to the long-term momentum.

Additionally, traders monitor the MACD histogram, which represents the difference between the MACD line and the signal line, to gauge the strength of the momentum. A widening histogram suggests that momentum is increasing, while a narrowing histogram indicates that momentum is decreasing.

Williams %R, a leading oscillator that pinpoints overbought and oversold conditions, similar to the RSI. These elements together provide a comprehensive picture of the market dynamics, equipping traders with essential tools for decision-making. It is based on the idea that prices tend to close near the highs in an uptrend and near the lows in a downtrend. The indicator is plotted as a line that fluctuates between 0 and -100 and is used to identify potential trend reversals and entry and exit points. A reading above -20 indicates overbought conditions, while a reading below -80 indicates oversold conditions.

Candlestick patterns are visual representations on a candlestick chart that offer valuable insights into an asset's potential price behavior. These patterns are formed by the arrangement of individual candlesticks, which reflect the open, high, low, and close prices of an asset within a specific time frame.

Notable candlestick patterns include:

1. **Hammer**: A bullish reversal pattern typically occurring at the end of a downtrend. It consists of a single candlestick with a small body and a long lower wick, suggesting that the price initially decreased, but then rebounded, indicating a possible trend reversal.

2. **Shooting Star**: A bearish reversal pattern usually appearing at the end of an uptrend. It

features a small body with a long upper wick, implying that the price initially increased, but eventually dropped, signaling a potential trend reversal.

3. **Engulfing Pattern**: A pattern consisting of two candlesticks, where the second candle's body completely engulfs the first candle's body. A bullish engulfing pattern occurs when a small bearish candle is followed by a larger bullish candle, suggesting a potential upward reversal. Conversely, a bearish engulfing pattern appears when a small bullish candle is followed by a larger bearish candle, indicating a possible downward reversal.

4. **Doji**: A pattern characterized by a candlestick with a very small or nonexistent body, signifying that the open and close prices are nearly equal. This pattern indicates market indecision and could signal a potential trend change, depending on the context in which it appears.

Additional Indicators:

- **Stochastic Oscillator**: A momentum-based indicator, the stochastic oscillator reveals potential overbought and oversold conditions by comparing an asset's closing price to its price range over a set time frame, plotted on a 0-100 scale. Readings above 80 suggest overbought territory, while those below 20 imply oversold conditions.

- **Fibonacci Retracements**: By applying the Fibonacci sequence, these horizontal lines signify potential support or resistance levels where an asset's price might encounter reversals or pauses.

- **Accumulation/Distribution**: This technical indicator gauges the flow of funds into and out of an asset by assigning values to each trading period based on price changes and trading volume. An upward trending A/D line indicates accumulation, while a downward trend indicates distribution.

- **Trend Strength**: Indicators like the Average Directional Index (ADX) assess the potency of a trend and help detect potential reversals by comparing the differences between two moving averages.

- **Ichimoku Cloud**: This indicator identifies potential support, resistance levels, and overall trends using multiple components, including the conversion line, base line, and cloud.

- **Bollinger Bands**: Designed to detect overbought and oversold conditions, Bollinger Bands plot two standard deviations above and below a moving average, adjusting with asset volatility.

- **Average True Range (ATR)**: This volatility measure calculates an asset's average true range (the difference between daily highs and lows) over a specific time frame, useful for setting stop-loss orders and identifying breakout trades.

Broadly, the world of technical analysis offers a multitude of indicators to help investors navigate market trends and make educated decisions. These tools represent just a small selection of the vast array available to traders and investors, allowing them to refine their market strategies and adeptly traverse the financial landscape.

Chart Patterns: Unveiling the Market's Intricate Dynamics

In the dominion of stock investing, chart analysis serves as an essential instrument to decipher the price fluctuations of individual stocks and overarching market trends.

At the core of chart analysis lies the concept of base patterns, which signify periods of consolidation in a stock's price prior to an upward or downward shift. Bases can encompass several weeks or even months, and discerning the various types of base patterns equips investors with the ability to pinpoint promising investment opportunities and effectively manage risk.

In this section, an assortment of chart patterns will be explored, emphasizing the distinct characteristics and signals associated with each pattern.

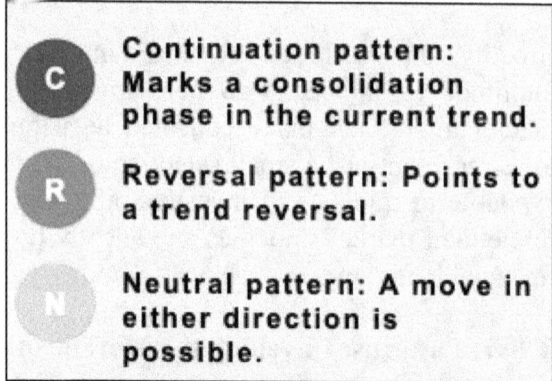

Figure: 19.6 Chart Patterns Legend

- **Cup with Handle**: This is one of the most common types of bases and is characterized by a rounded bottom and a short pullback known as the "handle." This base typically forms after a long uptrend and signals a potential continuation of the trend.

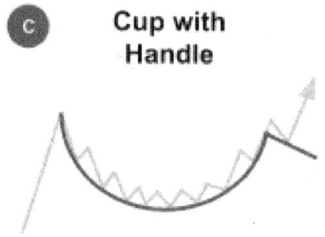

Figure: 19.7 Cup with Handle Base

- **Bullish Flag**: This pattern is characterized by a sharp price increase (the "flagpole"), followed by a consolidation period with a downward-sloping trendline (the "flag"). The consolidation period is typically short and narrow. A breakout above the trendline is often a strong buy signal.

c **Bullish Flag**

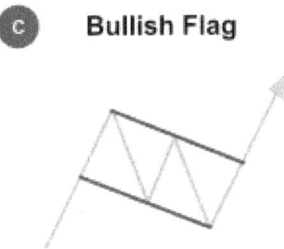

Figure: 19.8 Bullish Flag Base

- **Bearish Flag**: This pattern is the inverse of the bullish flag, with a sharp price decrease (the "flagpole") followed by a consolidation period with an upward-sloping trendline (the "flag"). The consolidation period is typically short and narrow. A breakout below the trendline is often a strong sell signal.

c **Bearish Flag**

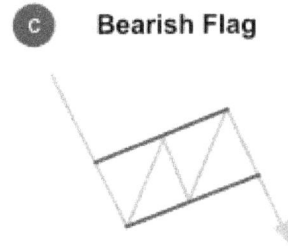

Figure: 19.9 Bearish Flag Base

- **Double Bottom**: This base pattern is characterized by two distinct lows that are separated by a peak in the middle. The second low is often slightly higher than the first, and the breakout from this base is typically accompanied by high volume.

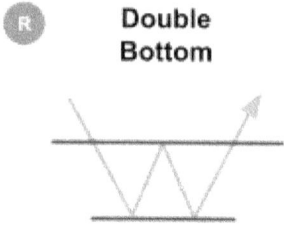

Figure: 19.10 Double Bottom Base

- **Double Top**: This base pattern is the opposite of the double bottom base and is characterized by two distinct highs that are separated by a trough in the middle. The second high is often slightly lower than the first, and the breakdown from this base is typically accompanied by high volume.

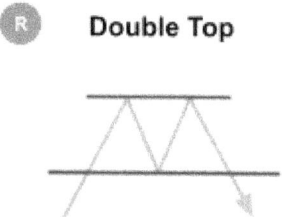

Figure: 19.11 Double Top Base

- **Flat (Rectangle)**: This base is characterized by a narrow and flat price range, often lasting for several weeks. The low and high points of this base are typically within 5% of each other, and the breakout from this base is often accompanied by strong volume.

Rectangle

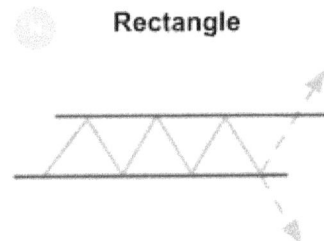

Figure: 19.12 Flat Base

- **Ascending Triangle**: This base is characterized by a series of higher lows and higher highs over a period of time. This pattern signals a gradual accumulation of the stock by buyers and can lead to a strong breakout.

Ascending Triangle

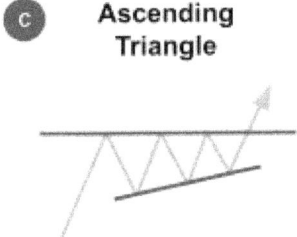

Figure: 19.13 Ascending Triangle Base

- **Descending Triangle**: This base is the opposite of the ascending base and is characterized by a series of lower highs and lower lows over a period of time. This pattern signals a gradual distribution of the stock by sellers and can lead to a strong breakdown.

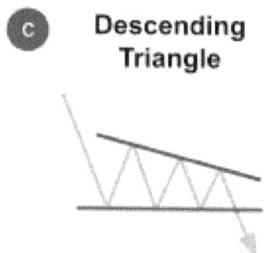

Figure: 19.14 Descending Triangle Base

- **Head and Shoulders**: This base is characterized by three distinct peaks, with the middle peak being the highest (the "head") and the two outer peaks being slightly lower (the "shoulders"). The consolidation period typically forms a downward-sloping neckline. A breakout below the neckline is often a strong sell signal.

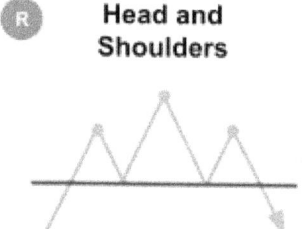

Figure: 19.15 Head and Shoulders Base

- **Inverse Head and Shoulders**: This base is the inverse of the head and shoulders base, with three distinct troughs instead of peaks. The middle trough is the lowest (the "head") and the two outer troughs are slightly higher (the "shoulders"). The consolidation period typically forms an upward-sloping neckline. A breakout above the neckline is often a strong buy signal.

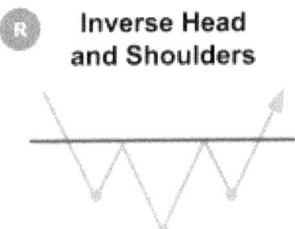

Figure: 19.16 Inverse Head and Shoulders Base

- **Bullish Pennant**: This pattern is similar to the bullish flag, with a sharp price increase followed by a consolidation period. However, in this case, the consolidation period is characterized by a symmetrical triangle pattern. A breakout above the triangle is often a strong buy signal.

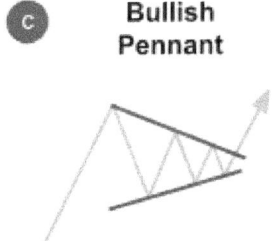

Figure: 19.17 Bullish Pennant Base

- **Bearish Pennant**: This pattern is the inverse of the bullish pennant, with a sharp price decrease followed by a consolidation period characterized by a symmetrical triangle pattern. A breakout below the triangle is often a strong sell signal.

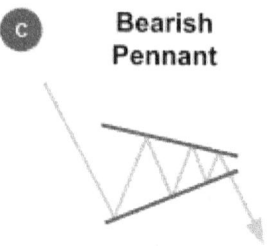

Figure: 19.18 Bearish Pennant Base

- **Bullish Channel**: This pattern is characterized by two upward-sloping parallel trendlines that contain the price movements. The trendlines are created by connecting the highs and lows of the consolidation period. A breakout above the upper trendline is often a strong buy signal.

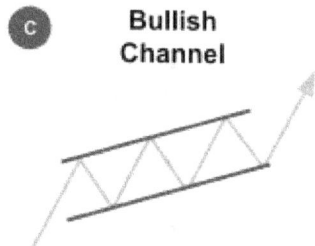

Figure: 19.19 Bullish Channel Base

- **Bearish Channel**: This pattern is the inverse of the bullish channel, with two downward-sloping parallel trendlines that contain the price movements. A breakout below the lower trendline is often a strong sell signal.

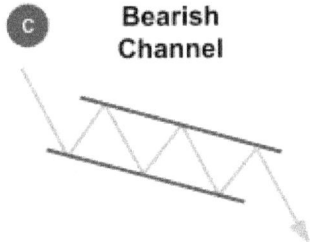

Figure: 19.20 Bearish Channel Base

- **Symmetrical Triangle**: This pattern is characterized by a consolidation period where the price movements are contained within two converging trendlines. The breakout direction is usually determined by the direction of the previous trend.

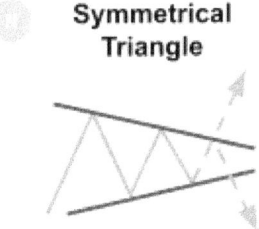

Figure: 19.21 Symmetrical Triangle Base

- **Diamond Top**: This pattern is characterized by a consolidation period that forms a diamond shape. The pattern is formed by connecting the highs and lows of the consolidation period. A breakout below the lower trendline is often a strong sell signal.

Figure: 19.22 Diamond Top Base

- **Rounding Bottom**: This pattern is characterized by a long and gradual price decline, followed by a gradual recovery to the original price level. The consolidation period is often broad and rounded, forming a "U" shape on the chart. The breakout from this base is typically accompanied by high volume.

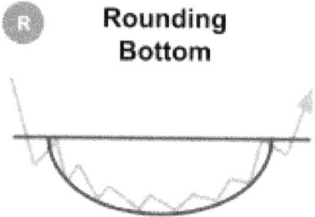

Figure: 19.23 Rounding Bottom Base

- **Falling Wedge**: This pattern is characterized by a consolidation period with a downward-sloping trendline and a flatter, upward-sloping trendline. The pattern is formed by connecting the highs and lows of the consolidation period. A breakout above the upper trendline is often a strong buy signal.

Falling Wedge

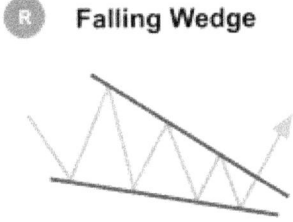

Figure: 19.24 Falling Wedge Base

- **Rising Wedge**: This pattern is the inverse of the falling wedge, with an upward-sloping trendline and a flatter, downward-sloping trendline. A breakout below the lower trendline is often a strong sell signal.

Rising Wedge

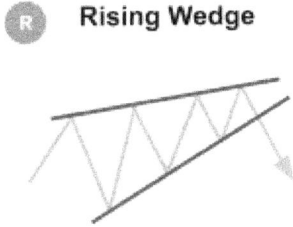

Figure: 19.25 Rising Wedge Base

- **Triple Top**: This pattern is characterized by three distinct peaks at approximately the same price level, with two troughs separating them. The consolidation period is typically broad and can be rectangular or rounded. A breakout below the support level is often a strong sell signal.

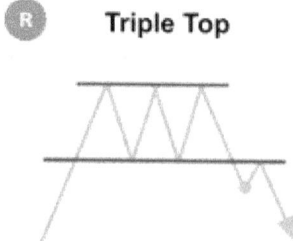

Figure: 19.26 Triple Top Base

- **Triple Bottom**: This pattern is the inverse of the triple top, with three distinct troughs at approximately the same price level, with two peaks separating them. A breakout above the resistance level is often a strong buy signal.

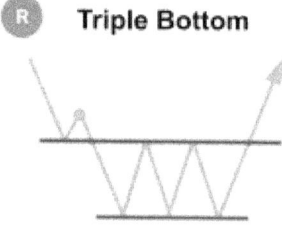

Figure: 19.27 Triple Bottom Base

- **Bump and Run**: This pattern is characterized by a steep price increase (the "bump"), followed by a period of consolidation with an upward-sloping trendline (the "run"). The trendline is often drawn below the price movements during the bump period.

Bump and Run

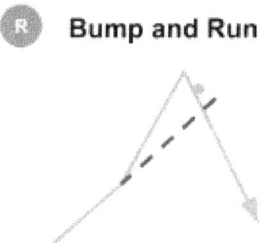

Figure: 19.28 Bump and Run Base

- **Megaphone**: Also known as the Broadening Formation, this pattern is characterized by two diverging trendlines, with the price action oscillating between them. The pattern is generally considered a reversal pattern, signaling an impending trend reversal. It is often observed during periods of heightened volatility and uncertainty in the markets. Traders look for a breakout beyond the trendlines to confirm the pattern and initiate trades in the direction of the breakout.

Megaphone

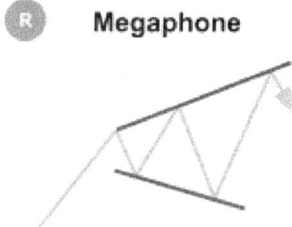

Figure: 19.29 Megaphone Base

In essence, mastering the diverse base patterns in chart analysis empowers investors to discern promising buying and selling opportunities while adeptly navigating risk in stocks or other investment instruments.

Orchestrating Technical Analysis and Essential Resources

Embarking on the journey of technical analysis involves a multifaceted and systematic approach to evaluating market data, with a particular focus on price and volume information. To excel in this discipline, investors must pay attention to several key considerations and leverage various essential resources.

Key Considerations:

- **Choose the appropriate time frame**: Determine the suitable time horizon for the analysis based on investment objectives and trading style. This could range from intraday charts for short-term traders to weekly or monthly charts for longer-term investors.

- **Determine the trend**: Identify the overall direction in which the price of an asset is moving. This can be achieved through the use of trend lines, moving averages, and other technical indicators.

- **Examine support and resistance levels**: Locate key price points where the asset has historically struggled to break through. These levels can act as potential entry or exit points for trades.

- **Evaluate chart patterns**: Recognize and interpret recognizable patterns, such as head and shoulders or triangles, which can provide clues about the asset's future price movements.

- **Employ technical indicators**: Utilize a variety of technical indicators, such as oscillators, volume, and momentum indicators, to gain a more complete picture of the asset's price action.

- **Consider the volume of trading**: The volume of trading in an asset can provide insight into the level of interest and participation in the market. Increasing volume may indicate a strengthening trend, while decreasing volume may suggest a weakening trend.

- **Use multiple technical analysis techniques**: Different technical analysis techniques may produce conflicting signals. By using a variety of techniques, you can get a more comprehensive view of the asset's price action and make more informed decisions.

- **Look for divergence**: Divergence occurs when the direction of the price action and the direction indicated by a technical indicator are at odds. This can be a potential sign of a trend reversal.

- **Use multiple chart types**: Different chart types, such as line charts, bar charts, and candlestick charts, can provide different perspectives on an asset's price action. Experiment with different chart types to find the one that works best for you.

- **Understand the role of liquidity**: The liquidity of an asset can impact its price action. Assets with high liquidity tend to have more stable prices, while assets with low liquidity may be more volatile.

- **Consider multiple assets**: Technical analysis can be applied to a variety of financial instruments, including stocks, currencies, cryptocurrencies, and commodities. By analyzing multiple assets, you may be able to identify correlations and diversify your portfolio.

- **Stay up-to-date**: The financial markets are constantly evolving, so it is important to stay up-to-date with the latest trends and developments. This includes keeping an eye on economic indicators and global events that may impact asset prices.

- **Keep an eye on news and fundamentals**: While technical analysis focuses on the price action of an asset, it is important to also consider any underlying fundamental factors that may impact the asset's price.

- **Develop a trading plan**: Use the insights gained from technical analysis to create a clear and structured plan for making trades. This plan should include entry and exit points, as well as risk management strategies.

- **Test and refine**: Continuously test and refine your technical analysis techniques to improve the accuracy of your trade predictions. This can be done through back testing and paper trading.

- **Keep a record of your trades**: It is important to keep track of your trades, including the reasons for making them and the results. This can help you analyze your performance and identify areas for improvement.

Essential Resources:

Investopedia: A leading comprehensive financial resource, Investopedia offers a plethora of articles, tutorials, and guides on technical analysis.

StockCharts: A versatile financial platform, StockCharts provides real-time stock prices, diverse charting tools, and valuable resources for technical analysis. In addition, ChartSchool, is a comprehensive educational resource offered by StockCharts, which covers a wide range of technical analysis concepts and tools.

TradingView: As a robust financial platform, TradingView delivers real-time stock and cryptocurrency prices, advanced charting tools, and a myriad of resources essential for in-depth technical analysis.

BabyPips: Designed with beginners in mind, BabyPips is a website that offers a user-friendly introduction to forex trading, encompassing a dedicated section on technical analysis.

Tradimo: A financial education platform, Tradimo presents a collection of courses on technical analysis, including a complimentary course on chart patterns.

FINVIZ: A popular financial visualization platform, which offers an array of powerful tools, including stock screeners, technical indicators, and interactive charts.

Summary

Technical analysis emerges as an elegant and vital discipline in the domain of finance and investment, focusing on the scrutiny of historical market information to predict forthcoming trends and price shifts. This method encompasses a variety of tools and techniques, including chart formations, moving averages, and oscillators, which allow for the extraction of insightful conclusions from price, volume, and sentiment data. Through recognizing persistent patterns and behaviors, technical analysis empowers market participants to refine their decision-making and augment their returns. In contrast to fundamental analysis, which aims to ascertain an asset's intrinsic worth, technical analysis is predicated on the notion that all pertinent data is inherently reflected in an asset's price, establishing it as an essential resource for traders and investors.

By delving into the world of technical analysis, one encounters a rich tapestry of key principles and methodologies. These include concepts such as support and resistance levels, trendlines, and a variety of chart styles, such as candlestick, bar, and line charts. Furthermore, an assortment of technical indicators, like the Relative Strength Index (RSI), Moving Average Convergence Divergence (MACD), and Bollinger Bands, serve as invaluable tools to uncover potential market opportunities and evaluate the vigor of prevailing trends. Importantly, the discipline also accentuates the value of risk management and trading psychology, highlighting the imperative nature of discipline, patience, and consistency in achieving enduring success. Through mastering the nuanced art and science of technical analysis, market participants can sharpen their decision-making process and elevate their performance amidst the ever-changing landscape of financial markets.

Chapter 20

Portfolio and Risk Management

Investment is a pursuit that calls for prudent deliberation and meticulous preparation to bring forth one's desired outcomes. The objectives of investing are diverse and unique, ranging from generating income and safeguarding one's capital to expanding one's wealth. To attain these goals, investors must gain a comprehensive understanding of the manifold investment strategies available, including portfolio and risk management, and the ways in which they can be harnessed to realize their desired outcomes. In this chapter, we shall delve into some of the most prevalent investment goals and strategies, focusing on portfolio and risk management, that investors can utilize to triumphantly navigate their investment journey.

Diversification

Diversification is a formidable risk management tactic that necessitates investing in an assortment of asset classes, industries, and geographic regions to diffuse risk and potentially amplify returns. The crux of diversification is that by embracing a broad range of investments, an investor can lessen the impact of any solitary investment's performance on their overall portfolio.

- Diversification has numerous advantages. For one, it can minimize the total risk of an investment portfolio. By investing in a diverse range of assets, an investor can mitigate the potential losses of a poorly performing investment, as the negative impact may be counteracted by the positive outcomes of others.

- In the long term, diversification can also potentially enhance returns. The reason being that different asset classes tend to perform differently at different times. By investing in a plethora of assets, an investor may capture the returns of numerous asset classes, potentially leading to higher overall returns.

- Diversifying an investment portfolio can be accomplished through various means, such as investing in stocks, bonds, and mutual funds, and diversifying across different industries, countries, and geographic regions.

- It is vital to keep in mind that diversification does not assure a profit or shield against loss, and it is still feasible to incur losses, even with a well-diversified portfolio.

- Over-diversification is another potential risk of diversification. This occurs when an investor spreads their investments too thin across too many different assets, making it difficult to achieve meaningful returns. It can also result in increased trading costs and a lack of focus in the portfolio. Therefore, it's important to find the right balance between diversification and concentration to maximize the potential benefits of diversification without sacrificing returns.

Rebalancing

Investment rebalancing is a mindful and strategic approach to maintaining a desired risk level and investment objective. It involves adjusting the allocation of assets in an investment portfolio on a periodic basis, to keep it in line with the investor's goals and risk appetite.

Rebalancing is typically accomplished by selling off some of the assets that have appreciated in value and using the proceeds to purchase additional shares of other assets that have not performed as well. This helps to ensure that the portfolio is not overly concentrated in any one asset or asset class.

There are several compelling reasons why an investor might choose to rebalance their portfolio:

- One of the primary reasons is to manage risk. By rebalancing regularly, an investor can mitigate the risk of losses if a particular asset class underperforms. This is because the portfolio will not be over-exposed to any one asset, which can lead to more significant losses.

- Rebalancing can also help an investor stay on track with their long-term investment goals. For instance, if an investor's portfolio has become too heavily weighted in a particular asset class, such as stocks, they may decide to sell some of their stock holdings and use the proceeds to purchase more bonds. This can help them achieve a more balanced portfolio, aligned with their risk tolerance and investment objectives.

Dollar-cost averaging

Dollar-cost averaging is a timeless investment strategy that emphasizes discipline and consistency. It involves investing a fixed amount of money at regular intervals, regardless of market conditions or investment prices.

- This method of investing can help to smooth out market volatility and potentially lower the average purchase price of an investment over time.

- By investing a fixed amount on a regular schedule, an investor is able to avoid making emotional decisions that may lead to buying high and selling low.

- Dollar-cost averaging is often used as a long-term investment strategy, as it takes time for the benefits to fully materialize. Over the long term, however, it can potentially lead to higher returns and lower risk.

- While dollar-cost averaging is not foolproof and does not guarantee a profit or protect against loss, it can be a prudent way for investors to systematically build up a portfolio over time.

- It is important to note that this strategy may not be suitable for short-term or speculative investments, as it is best suited for those with a long-term investment horizon.

Active management

Active management is a sophisticated investment approach that involves actively selecting and trading individual securities with the aim of outperforming a benchmark index. The goal of an active manager or investor is to generate higher returns than the market by conducting extensive research and analysis, identifying undervalued or mispriced securities, and making informed decisions based on their expectations of market conditions.

- Compared to passive management, which seeks to track a benchmark index, active management involves a more hands-on approach that requires a higher level of skill and expertise. However, this approach can be expensive as it involves paying for the services of a portfolio manager and incurring trading costs.

- The success of active management depends on the manager's ability to identify and capitalize on investment opportunities. It's worth noting that there's no guarantee that an active manager will outperform the market, and it is possible for an active manager to underperform the market.

- When considering active management as an investment strategy, investors should weigh the potential risks and fees associated with this approach against their investment objectives and risk tolerance.

Passive management

Passive management is a straightforward investment strategy that seeks to match the performance of a particular benchmark index such as the S&P 500, rather than attempting to beat it. This approach is commonly implemented through the use of index funds or ETFs, which are designed to track the performance of a specific index.

By minimizing the need for active trading and portfolio management, passive investing is generally considered to be a lower-cost investment strategy compared to active management.

- Passive investors typically seek to diversify their portfolio across a wide range of asset classes to mitigate risk and achieve broad market exposure.

- While passive investing may not offer the potential for high returns that active management can provide, it can offer long-term investors a simple and effective way to build wealth over time. However, it is important to note that the success of passive investing is dependent on the performance of the benchmark index, and market volatility and fluctuations can still impact investment returns. Therefore, it is important for investors to carefully consider their investment goals and risk tolerance before implementing a passive investment strategy.

Tactical asset allocation

Tactical asset allocation is an investment approach that involves actively managing a portfolio by making strategic changes to the allocation of assets based on an investor's views on market conditions. This allows investors to make deliberate adjustments to their portfolio, aiming to capitalize on potential opportunities and mitigate potential risks.

- Unlike passive management, tactical asset allocation seeks to outperform the overall market by making timely adjustments to the asset mix in a portfolio. This may involve using various investment tools such as futures, options, and ETFs to make quick and flexible changes.

- Tactical asset allocation is typically employed by investors with a high level of expertise and knowledge of the markets. However, it carries its own set of risks, such as incorrect market timing and transaction costs.

- Tactical asset allocation is best used as a complement to a long-term investment strategy, rather than as a standalone strategy.

- It is crucial for investors to carefully consider the potential risks and returns before implementing a tactical asset allocation strategy.

Practical Applications of Asset Allocation Strategies

Asset allocation is an essential facet that enables investors to customize their portfolio and exploit promising prospects while circumventing potential hazards.

Some instances that illustrate how investors utilize asset allocation:

- Adjusting the allocation of stocks, bonds, and cash: An astute investor who believes that the stock market is overvalued might seek to reduce their exposure to stocks and increase their allocation to bonds or cash. This can involve selling stocks and buying bonds or cash, or using futures or options to make these changes.

- Adjusting the allocation of domestic and international assets: An investor who foresees the weakening of the U.S. dollar may decide to increase their exposure to international assets, such as stocks or bonds denominated in foreign currencies. This can involve buying international assets or using currency forwards or futures to make the changes.

- Adjusting the allocation of growth and value stocks: Investors who favor value stocks over growth stocks might seek to adjust their portfolio allocation accordingly. This can involve buying value stocks and selling growth stocks, or using ETFs or other investment vehicles to make these changes.

- Adjusting the allocation of different sectors: A well-informed investor who expects a particular sector, such as technology or healthcare, to outperform the overall market might increase their allocation to that sector. This can involve buying individual stocks or sector-specific ETFs to make the necessary changes.

Useful resources for Portfolio and Risk Management

PortfolioVisualizer.com: Portfolio Visualizer offers a suite of free tools for portfolio analysis and optimization, risk analysis, asset correlation, and factor analysis. It also includes backtesting capabilities to assess the historical performance of different investment strategies.

Risk.net: As a comprehensive source for financial risk management news and analysis, Risk.net provides in-depth insight into credit, operational, and market risk, alongside regulations affecting these areas. While a portion of its content requires a subscription, it offers a selection of articles and features available for free, making it a valuable resource for understanding the risk landscape in financial markets.

OECD (Organisation for Economic Co-operation and Development) Statistics: The OECD provides a wealth of free international economic, social, and environmental data. This can be valuable for assessing global macroeconomic risks that could impact an investment portfolio.

AAII (American Association of Individual Investors): AAII provides educational materials and tools for investors, including resources on asset allocation, risk management, and portfolio construction. Though the website has a membership option, many resources are available for free.

MacroTrends.net: MacroTrends offers free access to long-term data for stocks, bonds, commodities, and economic indicators. This includes dividend history, price-earnings ratios, and other key financial metrics, useful for long-term portfolio management and risk analysis.

Federal Reserve Bank of New York's Center for Microeconomic Data: The center provides high-quality microeconomic data, including household debt and credit report, which can be useful for understanding trends.

Summary

Investment pursuits vary as the seeds of ambition within each investor differ, dictated by their financial objectives, risk appetite, and time horizon. To navigate the ever-evolving financial landscape, one may employ a myriad of investment strategies: diversification to mitigate risk and unlock potential gains, rebalancing to sustain optimal risk levels, dollar-cost averaging to shield from the vicissitudes of market volatility, and active or passive management styles that demand varying levels of skill and expertise.

A wise investor would be well-advised to ponder over their financial goals and risk appetite before embarking on their investment journey, for it is in this careful consideration that lies the key to realizing their aspirations.

Chapter 21

Paper Trading

The sphere of investing can appear daunting for novices; however, it need not be so. As with any intricate skill, practice paves the path to proficiency, and paper trading presents a secure and accessible avenue for cultivating one's abilities.

Paper trading, alternatively referred to as virtual or practice trading, embodies the simulation of real-world trading without risking tangible capital. It empowers individuals to explore various investment types and tactics through the use of simulated accounts. Employing virtual currency within these accounts ensures that any profits or losses accrued during trading activities remain unrealized in the real world.

Aspiring investors can harness the power of paper trading to deepen their comprehension of market intricacies, fine-tune their tactics, and ultimately, bolster their likelihood of triumph in the borough of investing. This proves particularly advantageous for fledgling investors endeavoring to master the fundamentals, as well as seasoned investors desiring to explore novel strategies or broaden their expertise within a particular domain.

Benefits

- Risk-free learning: Paper trading allows individuals to learn the mechanics of investing without the fear of losing real money. This can help to build confidence and experience before entering the world of real-world investing.

- Strategy development: By engaging in paper trading, investors can test out various strategies and investment types (e.g., stocks, options, futures, etc.) to find which work best for their unique risk appetite and goals.

- Emotional control: Paper trading helps to instill discipline and emotional control in investors, as they learn to make rational decisions based on market data rather than succumbing to impulsive reactions.

Disadvantages

- Lack of emotional attachment: Since no real money is at stake, the emotional experience of paper trading can be significantly different from real-world investing. This may lead to overconfidence or an inability to deal with the stress of actual market fluctuations.

- Imperfect simulation: Although paper trading can closely mimic real-world market conditions, it cannot account for certain factors, such as slippage or liquidity, which may impact the outcomes of trades in a live environment.

- Complacency: The risk-free nature of paper trading can foster a sense of complacency, causing investors to underestimate the real risks associated with investing.

Delving into Performance Assessment and Embracing Lessons Learned

One of the most paramount aspects of paper trading lies in the opportunity to appraise performance and assimilate lessons from missteps without sustaining tangible financial setbacks. By consistently scrutinizing and dissecting their trades, investors can discern patterns in their decision-making processes and pinpoint areas necessitating improvement. This cycle of introspection and learning is vital for cultivating the requisite skills and mindset for triumph in the sphere of real-world investing.

To effectively evaluate performance, investors should contemplate the following:

Monitoring performance metrics: Investors ought to keep a close watch on essential performance indicators, such as win/loss ratio, average gain/loss, and comprehensive portfolio returns. These metrics can yield invaluable insights into the strengths and shortcomings of their strategies.

Journaling trades: By maintaining an exhaustive trade journal, investors can document their rationale and decision-making for each trade. This practice permits them to revisit past choices, detect patterns or biases, and extract lessons from both prosperous and unsuccessful trades.

Soliciting feedback and education: Paper trading can be further augmented by seeking counsel from seasoned investors or participating in online investment communities. Additionally, investors should seize the opportunity to utilize educational resources available on paper trading platforms or from reputable sources to expand their knowledge and refine their skills.

Navigating the Transition from Paper Trading to Real-World Investing

Although paper trading offers inestimable practice and learning prospects, investors will eventually need to embrace the world of real-world investing. Navigating this transition can be daunting; however, by implementing the lessons acquired through paper trading, investors can enhance their likelihood of success.

Here are some recommendations for facilitating a seamless transition:

Commencing with modesty: When shifting to real-world investing, it is judicious to initiate with a small amount of capital. This strategy enables investors to acclimate to the emotional facets of investing and the mechanics of their chosen platform without jeopardizing substantial sums.

Upholding discipline: The strategies and techniques refined during paper trading must be consistently employed in real-world investing. Preserving the same degree of discipline and emotional regulation is critical for sustained success.

Adapting and evolving: Real-world investing will inevitably present novel challenges and experiences that were not encountered during paper trading. Investors should remain receptive to learning from these experiences, adjusting their strategies accordingly, and continuously striving to enhance their skills.

Paper Trading Scenarios on Renowned Platforms

Example 1: Diversifying a Portfolio by utilizing **Thinkorswim**

Emily, a novice investor, has been studying the stock market and wishes to create a diverse portfolio to minimize risk. She decides to use Thinkorswim's paper trading feature to practice building her portfolio. Emily creates a virtual account on Thinkorswim and begins researching various stocks, ETFs, and bonds. After identifying a mix of assets across different sectors and risk levels, she allocates her virtual funds accordingly. Over time, she monitors her portfolio's performance, using the platform's advanced charting and analysis tools to make adjustments as needed.

Example 2: Exploring Options Trading with **E*TRADE**

Jack, an experienced stock investor, has become interested in options trading as a means to generate additional income and hedge his existing stock positions. However, he is not yet confident in his understanding of options strategies. Jack opens a paper trading account with E*TRADE and uses the platform's educational resources to familiarize himself with various options strategies, such as covered calls and iron condors. He then practices implementing these strategies with virtual money, adjusting his approach based on the outcomes and refining his skills over time.

Example 3: Developing a Swing Trading Strategy with **Webull**

Michael, an aspiring swing trader, wants to capitalize on short-term price movements by developing a solid swing trading strategy. He chooses Webull, a popular paper trading platform, to practice and refine his trading approach. Upon creating a virtual account, Michael begins researching potential trades using Webull's extensive charting tools and fundamental analysis features. As he identifies and executes trades based on his strategy, he meticulously tracks their performance and makes adjustments as necessary to improve his accuracy and risk management.

Example 4: Building a Balanced Portfolio with **Investopedia**

Kevin, a recent college graduate, is eager to begin investing but has limited knowledge of the stock market. He decides to use Investopedia's Stock Simulator to learn the ropes before investing his real savings. Kevin creates a virtual account on the Investopedia Stock Simulator and starts researching stocks, ETFs, and mutual funds. He gradually builds a balanced portfolio that aligns with his long-term financial goals and risk tolerance. As he monitors the performance of his simulated portfolio over time, he gains valuable insights into market dynamics and portfolio management.

Summary

In conclusion, paper trading serves as an invaluable instrument for budding investors, offering a sanctuary where they can meticulously hone their skills, explore a myriad of strategies, and deepen their grasp of the enigmatic tapestry of market complexities. By engaging with distinguished platforms and immersing themselves in a diverse array of investment scenarios, investors can transmute their theoretical acumen into tangible expertise, cultivate emotional equilibrium, and proficiently assess their performance. The wisdom gleaned from this simulated domain of investing can be carried forth into the purview of real-world investing, establishing a robust foundation for lasting financial triumph.

As individuals traverse the odyssey from paper trading to real-world investing, it is imperative to uphold the discipline, adaptability, and unwavering dedication to continuous learning acquired through these practice sessions. By initiating their journey with modest capital, employing the techniques polished during paper trading, and remaining open to the valuable insights offered by the ever-evolving landscape of investing, individuals can seamlessly transition into the tangible sphere of finance. This dynamic and enriching process will empower investors to actualize their financial aspirations while progressively mastering the intricate interplay of art and science inherent in the world of investing.

Part VI

Getting Started

Chapter 22

Opening a Trading Account

With the plethora of investment opportunities available in today's global market, having a reliable and efficient trading account is essential for any aspiring investor.

In a world where financial markets are interconnected and easily accessible through the internet, investors have the unique opportunity to diversify their portfolios across a multitude of assets and geographical locations. This vast landscape of investment choices requires a clear understanding of the intricacies involved in setting up a trading account.

Choosing the Right Account Features and Understanding Fees

When opening a trading account, it is essential to consider the various features and fees associated with the account, as they can significantly impact your overall trading experience and profitability.

Account Features to Consider:

Trading Platform: The trading platform is the interface through which you execute trades and manage your investments. It is crucial to choose a trading platform that is user-friendly, reliable, and offers the tools and features you need to analyze and execute your trades effectively.

Customer Support*:* Excellent customer support is vital, as it ensures that you have access to assistance when needed. Consider the availability, responsiveness, and quality of the brokerage's customer support when selecting a trading account.

Research and Analysis Tools*:* Many brokerages offer research and analysis tools to help investors make informed decisions. Look for a trading account that provides access to high-quality market research, news, and analytical tools to support your investment strategy.

Order Types*:* The availability of various order types can give you greater control over your trades. Ensure that the trading account you choose offers a range of order types, such as market, limit, stop, and trailing stop orders.

Educational Resources*:* For beginners and experienced investors alike, educational resources can be invaluable in developing and refining trading strategies. Choose a trading account that offers access to comprehensive educational materials, such as articles, webinars, or video courses.

Reputation and regulation*:* Ensure that the brokerage is regulated by a reputable financial authority and has a solid reputation within the industry. This will provide you with added protection and peace of mind.

Understanding Fees and Commissions

Different brokerages charge various fees and commissions, which can impact your investment returns. Be sure to understand and compare the fee structures of different trading accounts before making a decision:

- **Trading Commissions**: Brokerages may charge commissions for each trade executed on their platform. These commissions can be fixed or variable, based on the size and type of the trade.

- **Account Maintenance Fees**: Some brokerages charge an annual or monthly fee for maintaining your trading account, while others may waive this fee if you meet specific requirements, such as maintaining a minimum account balance.

- **Inactivity Fees**: If you do not trade frequently, you may be subject to inactivity fees, which are charged when your account does not meet a minimum trading volume or frequency.

- **Margin Interest**: If you choose to trade on margin, you will need to pay interest on the borrowed funds. The interest rate and calculation method can vary between brokerages.

- **Foreign Exchange Fees**: If you plan to trade in international markets, you may be subject to foreign exchange fees when converting currencies.

- **Withdrawal Fees**: Some brokerages charge a fee for withdrawing funds from your trading account.

This fee can vary depending on the withdrawal method and frequency.

Selecting the right account features and understanding the associated fees is crucial when opening a trading account. By carefully considering your needs and preferences, and comparing different brokerages' offerings, you can choose a trading account that aligns with your investment goals and strategy.

Different Accounts for Different Investment Vehicles in Different Countries

United States: In the US, investors can open various types of trading accounts, such as individual, joint, corporate, custodial, or retirement accounts like Individual Retirement Accounts (IRAs) or 401(k) plans. These accounts can be used to invest in stocks, bonds, mutual funds, ETFs, options, and futures.

Canada: The Canadian investment landscape offers a variety of investment vehicles and account types for investors. In Canada, investors can open individual, joint, corporate, custodial, or tax-advantaged accounts like Registered Retirement Savings Plans (RRSPs), Tax-Free Savings Accounts (TFSAs), and Registered Education Savings Plans (RESPs). These accounts are designed to help Canadians save for specific financial goals, such as retirement or education expenses, and offer unique tax benefits.

European Union: In the EU, investors have access to a range of investment vehicles similar to those in the US, and can open accounts like individual, joint, corporate, custodial, or retirement accounts. Additionally, some countries offer tax-advantaged accounts like the UK's Individual Savings Accounts (ISAs) or France's Plan d'Épargne en Actions (PEA).

Asia: In Asian countries, investors can also access various investment vehicles and account types. For instance, in China, investors can open A-share and B-share accounts for trading domestic and foreign stocks, respectively. In India, investors can use Demat accounts to trade stocks, bonds, mutual funds, and ETFs.

Different types of trading accounts cater to the diverse needs of investors:

- *Individual account:* Owned and managed by a single individual.
- *Joint account:* Owned and managed by two or more individuals.
- *Corporate account:* Owned and managed by a corporation or business.
- *Custodial account:* Owned by a minor (under the age of 18) and managed by an adult (the custodian).
- *Trust account:* Owned by a trust and managed by a trustee.

Some trading accounts also provide tax advantages:

- *Tax-Free Savings Account (TFSA):* Available in some countries (e.g., Canada), allowing investors to buy and sell financial instruments within specific tax-advantaged rules.
- *Individual Retirement Account (IRA):* A retirement account offering tax advantages.
- *401(k) plan:* A retirement savings plan offered by employers in the United States, allowing

employees to contribute a portion of their salary to a tax-advantaged investment account.

Finally, **Margin accounts** allow investors to borrow money from a broker to buy securities, with the securities in the account serving as collateral.

Margin accounts carry a higher level of risk than cash accounts, and investors should carefully consider the risks and rewards before opening one. It is also essential for investors to monitor their margin account balance and be prepared to add additional funds or sell securities if necessary to maintain the required margin level.

Verifying Your Trading Account

Financial regulatory authorities require brokerages to follow a Know Your Customer (KYC) process, which involves verifying the identity of their clients. This process helps prevent fraud, money laundering, and other illegal activities. The verification process typically includes the following steps:

Proof of Identity: You will need to provide a valid government-issued identification document (e.g., passport, driver's license, or national ID card) to verify your identity.

Proof of Address: Brokerages require proof of your residential address, which can be demonstrated through utility bills, bank statements, or government-issued documents.

Additional Verification: In some cases, brokerages may request additional documents, such as tax identification numbers, employment information, or financial statements, to complete the verification process.

Once you have submitted the required documents, the brokerage will review them and confirm your account's verification status. This process may take a few business days to complete, depending on the brokerage's procedures and workload.

Funding Your Trading Account

After successfully opening a trading account, the next essential step in your trading journey is to fund and verify the account. Funding and verifying your trading account ensures that you have the necessary capital to initiate trades, while also adhering to the regulatory requirements set forth by financial authorities.

Bank Transfers: One of the most common methods of funding your trading account is through bank transfers. You can initiate a transfer from your bank account to your brokerage account, which typically takes a few business days to process. Be aware of any fees associated with bank transfers, as these may vary depending on your bank and brokerage.

Credit and Debit Cards: Many brokerages accept credit and debit card payments for funding trading accounts. This method is generally faster than bank transfers, but may come with higher fees and transaction limits.

Electronic Wallets: Some brokerages allow funding through electronic wallets (e.g., PayPal, Skrill, or Neteller). These services offer a quick and convenient way to transfer funds, although may also come with associated fees and restrictions.

Checks and Money Orders: In some cases, brokerages may accept checks or money orders as a funding method. While this option may be slower than electronic methods, it can be a suitable choice for investors who prefer traditional payment methods.

Account Security and Maintenance

Maintaining the security of your trading account is crucial to protect your personal information and financial assets. Consider the following best practices to ensure account security:

- *Strong Passwords:* Create a unique, complex password (minimum 14 characters) for your trading account, and avoid using the same password across multiple accounts.
- *Two-Factor Authentication (2FA):* Enable 2FA, if available, to add an extra layer of security to your account. This usually involves verifying your identity through a secondary device, such as a smartphone, when logging in.
- *Regular Monitoring:* Frequently review your account activity and statements to identify any discrepancies or unauthorized transactions.
- *Software Updates:* Keep your devices and security software up-to-date to protect against potential threats.

Summary

The obscure process of opening a trading account necessitates a conscientious evaluation of numerous factors, encompassing account features and the fees intertwined with them. By assiduously scrutinizing the trading platform, customer support, research and analysis tools, order types, educational resources, and the labyrinth of fee structures, you can deftly select an account that aligns harmoniously with your distinct needs and preferences.

As you commence your voyage into the captivating dominion of finance, always bear in mind the paramount importance of fastidiously selecting the ideal account. By devoting time and unwavering effort to comprehend the subtleties of various account offerings, you construct an unshakable foundation for a seamless and gratifying trading experience.

Chapter 23

Order Execution

A trading order constitutes an essential component in an investor's arsenal, playing a pivotal role in enabling the acquisition or divestment of financial instruments, including stocks, bonds, and other securities. Execution of these orders can be accomplished through traditional brokerage firms or contemporary online brokers, both of which provide a vast array of choices designed to cater to the distinct preferences and strategies of individual investors.

Order execution refers to the process by which a trading order is completed. When an investor submits an order to buy or sell a financial instrument, the brokerage firm or online broker routes the order to the appropriate exchange or market maker for execution. The speed and efficiency of order execution can vary depending on the broker, trading platform, and market conditions.

With the rapid advancement of technology and the increasing accessibility of financial markets, a diverse selection of order types has emerged, each offering its unique benefits and potential drawbacks. As a result, investors are empowered to make informed decisions that align with their risk tolerance, investment goals, and market conditions. By leveraging the appropriate order type, investors can not only optimize their trading efficiency but also enhance their overall portfolio performance.

Types of Orders

Market Order: Seizing Opportunities in Real-Time

A market order is a swift and direct request to buy or sell a financial instrument at the prevailing market price. This type of order is designed to capture opportunities as they arise, ensuring rapid execution. However, due to the inherent fluctuations of the market, the final price may deviate from the investor's initial target.

Advantages:
> Expedient execution for seizing time-sensitive opportunities.
> Uncomplicated process that caters to investors seeking simplicity.

Disadvantages:
> Potential price discrepancies due to market volatility.
> Unpredictable market conditions that may impact order fulfillment.

Expert Insight: Investors are advised to exercise caution when placing market orders due to their susceptibility to price volatility.

Limit orders, which enable investors to designate specific buy or sell prices, are often a more prudent alternative.

Limit Order: Emphasising Control Over Your Transactions

A limit order empowers investors to assert greater control over their transactions by stipulating the buying or selling of financial instruments at a specified price or better. This enhanced control ensures that investors achieve their desired transaction prices. However, limit orders are not guaranteed to be executed and may only be partially filled if the desired price is unattainable.

Advantages:

Price precision that offers greater control over transactions.

Partial fill potential that enables investors to capitalize on available opportunities.

Disadvantages:

No execution guarantee, which may result in missed opportunities.

Execution risk arising from significant market fluctuation.

Stop-Loss Order: Safeguarding Your Investments

A stop-loss order is a protective measure designed to automatically sell a financial instrument when it reaches a predetermined price (the stop price). This order type aims to mitigate potential losses on an investor's position by establishing a predefined exit point.

Advantages:

Effective risk management that shields investments from excessive losses.

Emotional detachment from trading decisions, promoting rational decision-making.

Disadvantages:

Execution risk due to rapid price movements or wide bid-ask spreads.
Gap risk, where significant price changes may bypass the stop price.

Stop-Limit Order: Combining the Best of Both Worlds

A stop-limit order merges the features of stop-loss and limit orders, enabling investors to buy or sell financial instruments when they reach a specific stop price but only at the designated limit price or better. This hybrid approach provides investors with enhanced control over transaction prices while maintaining a predefined exit strategy.

Advantages:
Price control that offers a balanced approach to trading.
Partial fill potential that allows investors to capture available opportunities.
Disadvantages:
No execution guarantee, which may result in missed opportunities.
Execution risk arising from significant market fluctuations.

Trailing Stop Order: Locking in Profits and Managing Risks

A trailing stop order dynamically adjusts the stop price as the market price of a financial instrument moves, allowing investors to secure profits or limit potential losses adaptively. This order type accommodates market fluctuations, ensuring that investors can react to changing conditions while maintaining a safety net.

Advantages:
Profit protection that adapts to market fluctuations, locking in gains.
Dynamic risk management that adjusts to market movements.
Disadvantages:
Execution risk due to rapid price movements or wide bid-ask spreads.
Gap risk, where significant price changes may bypass the stop price.

Good-Till-Cancelled (GTC) Order: Persistence in Pursuit of Opportunities

A GTC order is a persistent trading order that remains active until either the investor cancels it or it is executed. This order type allows investors to maintain their desired transaction parameters until favorable market conditions arise.

Advantages:
Flexibility afforded by the indefinite lifespan of the order.
Price control that ensures transactions adhere to investor preferences.
Disadvantages:
Execution risk arising from significant market fluctuations.
Forgotten orders that may lead to unexpected trades or missed opportunities.

Immediate-or-Cancel (IOC) Order: The Need for Speed

An IOC order demands immediate execution or cancellation of any unfilled portion of the order. This order type is ideal for investors seeking rapid entry or exit from a position, prioritizing speed over flexibility.

Advantages:
Quick execution that caters to time-sensitive trading strategies.
Partial fill potential that allows investors to capitalize on available opportunities.
Disadvantages:
No execution guarantee, which may result in missed opportunities.
Execution risk arising from significant market fluctuations.

Day Order: Seizing the Day's Opportunities

A day order is a trading order that expires at the end of the trading day if it is not executed. This order type is suitable for investors who wish to take advantage of short-term market fluctuations and are not interested in maintaining the order beyond the trading day.

Advantages:
Emphasis on short-term trading opportunities.
Automatic expiration prevents the order from lingering past the trading day.
Disadvantages:
Limited time frame may result in missed opportunities.
Incomplete orders at the end of the trading day.

All-or-None (AON) Order: A Singular Focus

An AON order is a trading order that requires the

entire order to be executed or not executed at all. This order type appeals to investors who prioritize complete order fulfillment and are willing to forgo partial fills or adjustable prices.

Advantages:
  Guarantees full order execution or none at all.
  Eliminates the risk of partial fills that may impact investment strategies.
Disadvantages:
  Reduced flexibility due to the stringent order requirements.
  No execution guarantee, which may result in missed opportunities.

Iceberg Order: Concealing Large Orders

An iceberg order is a large trading order that is divided into smaller, visible portions to hide the true size of the order from the market. This order type is beneficial for institutional investors and large traders who wish to minimize the market impact of their substantial orders.

Advantages:
  Minimizes market impact of sizable orders.
  Conceals true order size, preventing price manipulation.
Disadvantages:
  Increased complexity in managing multiple smaller orders.
  Potential for incomplete execution of the entire large order.

One-Cancels-the-Other (OCO) Order: A Contingent Strategy

An OCO order is a pair of orders, typically a limit order and a stop order, where the execution of one order automatically cancels the other order. This order type is ideal for investors who wish to establish a predetermined exit strategy for their positions, allowing them to profit from favorable market conditions or limit losses during unfavorable ones.

Advantages:
> Provides a balanced exit strategy by incorporating both profit-taking and risk management.
> Automatic cancellation of the other order reduces the need for constant monitoring.

Disadvantages:
> Execution risk due to the reliance on the specific conditions of each order type.
> Cancellation of one order may lead to missed opportunities in a rapidly changing market.

Slippage, and Market Hours

Understanding the concept of slippage, and market hours is crucial for investors seeking to optimize their trading performance.

Slippage

Slippage is the difference between the investor's desired price and the actual price at which the order is executed. It can occur due to several factors, including market volatility, liquidity, and the speed of order execution. Slippage can lead to either favorable or unfavorable outcomes, depending on whether the execution price is better or worse than the investor's desired price.

Example: Envision an investor, Jane, who is interested in purchasing shares of XYZ Corp. She notices that the current market price is $50 per share and decides to place a market order for 100 shares. However, due to heightened market volatility, the price of XYZ Corp. shares experiences rapid fluctuations. By the time her order reaches the market for execution, the price per share has risen to $50.25. Consequently, Jane's order is filled at this higher price, resulting in a slippage of $0.25 per share, or an additional $25 for the entire order (100 shares × $0.25 = $25). In this instance, the slippage has led to an unfavorable outcome for Jane, as she paid more than her initially desired price.

Conversely, if Jane were selling shares of XYZ Corp. instead of buying them, and the execution price rose to $50.25 from her desired price of $50, the slippage would work in her favor. In this case, she would receive an additional $0.25 per share in proceeds from the sale.

To minimize the impact of slippage on trading performance, investors can:

- Use limit orders, which specify the maximum price they are willing to pay when buying, or the minimum price they are willing to accept when selling.
- Avoid placing orders during periods of high volatility, as rapid price fluctuations can increase the likelihood of slippage.
- Select a broker with a reputation for fast and efficient order execution.

Market Hours and Trading Sessions

Financial markets operate during specific hours, which can impact the execution and pricing of trading orders. It is essential for investors to understand the trading hours for the markets in which they are active, as well as the implications of trading during different sessions.

The major stock exchanges, such as the New York Stock Exchange (NYSE) and the Nasdaq, operate during regular market hours, typically from 9:30 a.m. to 4:00 p.m. Eastern Time (ET). However, there are also pre-market and after-hours trading sessions that occur before and after the regular market hours.

Pre-market trading typically takes place between 4:00 a.m. and 9:30 a.m. ET, while after-hours trading occurs between 4:00 p.m. and 8:00 p.m. ET. Trading during these extended hours can offer opportunities to capitalize on news events or other market developments, but it also carries potential risks, such as lower liquidity and wider bid-ask spreads, which can impact order execution and pricing.

Summary

A profound comprehension of the various order types, their execution and nuances are indispensable for investors seeking to excel in the financial markets. By acquainting themselves with the intricacies of the diverse order types, investors can judiciously choose the one that aligns with their specific objectives. Furthermore, a thorough understanding of concepts such as slippage, market hours, and trade execution strategies enables them to minimize risks and capitalize on potential gains.

Equally significant is the investors' awareness of the implications associated with trading during distinct market sessions, including pre-market and after-hours trading. While these sessions present unique opportunities, they also harbor inherent risks. Possessing a firm grasp of these trading aspects not only empowers investors to make well-informed decisions but also furnishes them with the necessary tools to thrive in the dynamic world of financial markets.

Chapter 24

Conclusion

As the curtains draw on this odyssey of investing wisdom, let us reflect on the harmonious melody of the lessons learned. Each note, a principle to guide us; each chord, a testament to the importance of remaining steadfast and disciplined in our financial pursuits.

Our journey may be fraught with challenges and tempests, but let the resounding echoes of these guiding principles steer us towards the shores of financial security:

Cultivate the habit of regular saving and investing, allowing the power of compounding to work its magic and accelerate your wealth growth over time.

Develop a keen understanding of your own behavioral biases, and strive to overcome these tendencies to make more objective and rational investment decisions.

Establish a solid financial foundation by creating an emergency fund and developing a comprehensive plan that encompasses all aspects of your financial life.

Enhance your financial acumen by learning about investing and staying informed, empowering you to make informed decisions and steer clear of scams.

Seek the expertise of a professional financial advisor, but diligently research and evaluate their background and qualifications to ensure a fruitful partnership.

Build a diversified portfolio across assets, sectors, and regions to mitigate risk, while avoiding excessive diversification.

Embrace the principle of value investing by seeking undervalued assets with strong fundamentals, poised for long-term appreciation and stability.

Manage risk effectively by exercising discipline, and aligning your investment strategy with your objectives, risk tolerance, and time horizon.

Continuously re-evaluate and adjust your portfolio to accommodate life's changing circumstances, ensuring that your investment strategy remains attuned to your evolving needs and goals.

Stay mindful of fees and expenses, regularly comparing options and choosing cost-efficient investments to preserve your wealth over time.

Utilize tax-advantaged accounts and investment vehicles to optimize your financial returns and minimize the impact of taxes on your wealth accumulation.

Foster a spirit of resilience and adaptability in the face of market volatility, equipping yourself to navigate unforeseen challenges and seize emerging opportunities.

Nurture a mindset of financial stewardship, making responsible and sustainable investment choices that align with your values and contribute positively to society and the environment.

Remain patient concentrating on your long-term financial goals, and resist being swayed by short-term market fluctuations.

Venturing on the path to successful investing is no easy feat, but with discipline and patience, it is a journey worth taking. It begins with a deep understanding of your financial goals and risk appetite, arming you with the knowledge to make informed decisions, even when the markets are turbulent.

One of the keys to unlocking success lies in keeping your eyes trained on the long-term horizon. Investing is a marathon, a journey of endurance rather than speed, and impulsive decisions based on short-term market movements can lead you astray.

As you embark on your own financial symphony, may the resonant chords of these investment axioms reverberate in the chambers of your heart. With patience, discipline, and unwavering resolve, you shall compose the score of your financial triumph, culminating in a grand finale of a prosperous future.